Intellectual Property Law and Litigation,
Second Edition

by Edward F. O'Connor

TORT TRIAL & INSURANCE PRACTICE

Defending Liberty
Pursuing Justice

Cover design by ABA Publishing.

The materials contained herein represent the opinions and views of the authors and/or the editors, and should not be construed to be the views or opinions of the law firms or companies with whom such persons are in partnership with, associated with, or employed by, nor of the American Bar Association or the Tort Trial and Insurance Practice Section unless adopted pursuant to the bylaws of the Association.

Nothing contained in this book is to be considered as the rendering of legal advice, either generally or in connection with any specific issue or case. Nor do these materials purport to explain or interpret any specific bond or policy , or any provisions thereof, issued by any particular insurance company, or to render insurance or other professional advice. Readers are responsible for obtaining advice from their own lawyer or other professional. This book and any forms and agreements herein are intended for educational and informational purposes only.

© 2003 American Bar Association. All rights reserved.
Printed in the United States of America.

07 06 05 04 03 5 4 3 2 1

Library of Congress Cataloging-in-Publication Data

O'Connor, Edward F., 1944-
Intellectual property law and litigation, second edition / by Edward F. O'Connor.— 2nd ed.
        p. cm.
Rev. ed. of: A primer on intellectual property law and patent litigation / Edward F. O'Connor. c1997.
    ISBN 1-59031-230-9 (pbk.)
    1. Intellectual property—United States. 2. Patent suits—United States. 3. Antitrust law—United States. I. O'Connor, Edward F., 1944- Primer on intellectual property law and patent litigation. II. Title.

KF2980.O36 2003
346.7304'8—dc21   2003011784

Contents

Introduction

This book is a sequel to my first highly popular and widely read *A Primer on Intellectual Property Law and Patent Litigation.*[1] Both my mother and the other person who read it said it wasn't too bad.

My previous book was primarily intended as a primer for lawyers and businessmen who may not specialize in intellectual property but who need to have an understanding of the rudimentary fundamentals. Neither my previous book, nor this book is intended for those who practice regularly in this area of the law. (Although there may be something of value, even for the specialist, in terms of individual cases and issues with which I have dealt or about which I have some knowledge.)

The American Bar Association has asked me to write a sequel primarily because there have been substantial changes in the law since then. This book will attempt to discuss those developments and changes. In addition, however, I have included more detailed discussions of antitrust and related litigation, while also delving into areas of the law I neglected in my previous book—software copyright litigation in particular.

A word of warning: This is not intended to be a reference book. By the time this book is printed, much of it is likely to be obsolete. That is because the Court of Appeals for the Federal Circuit issues something like 100 precedent-setting decisions in a year. Also, this book contains a substantial amount of anecdotal material. The reason for that is that this provides me with the opportunity to illustrate, by example, certain principals and issues that would otherwise be purely theoretical. Finally, since I'm relatively sure you didn't buy my first book (which, coincidentally, was my last book) and because I am fundamentally lazy, I have included wholesale chapters from my first (my last) book. Therefore, if you have shelled out the big bucks for this book, you don't have to shell out more big bucks for an obsolete, uninteresting, uninviting, and all-around bad book. You can get all of that right here.

---

1. With a riveting title like that, how could it be anything other than a best-seller?

You will note that there are very few citations in this book. That is done deliberately. For citations to specific principles of intellectual property and antitrust law, please refer to *Chisum on Patents; McCarthy on Trademarks; Nimmer on Copyrights*; and *Areeda on Anti-Trust*. This book is about concepts and ideas. That does not mean that we will not, from time to time, cite specific cases. These citations will occur in the context of a discussion about those particular cases and the manner in which they have changed the landscape of intellectual property and/or antitrust law and litigation. For example, we will be discussing the impact of *Vitronics v. Conceptronics, Inc.,* 90 F.3d 1576 (Fed. Cir. 1996); *Gentry Gallery, Inc. v. Berkline Corp.,* 134 F.3d 1473 (Fed. Cir. 1998); *Reiffin v. Microsoft,* 214 F.3d 1342 (Fed. Cir., 2000); *Symbol Techs. Inc. v. Lemelson Med.,* 277 F.3d 1361 (Fed. Cir. 2002); and *Festo Corp. v. Shoketsu Kinzoku Kogyo Kabushiki Co.,* 122 S. Ct. 1831 (2002) Some cases cited herein may not be of significant value as authorities, but may be cases with which I am familiar (having tried them) or otherwise been involved in and that I hope will illustrate a point I am trying to make.

What's Changed?

Since my last book, the patent statutes have been rewritten and the Supreme Court's decision in *Warner Jenkinson Co., Inc. v. Hilton Davis Chemical Co.,* 520 U.S. 17 (1997) was issued. The Supreme Court and the Court of Appeals for the Federal Circuit (CAFC) have engaged in an unseemly and undignified tug of war over the doctrine of equivalents in *Festo Corp. v. Shoketsu Kinzoku Kogyo Kabushiki Co.,* 122 S. Ct 1831 (2002). The CAFC, in *Vitronics Corp. v. Conceptronics, Inc.,* 90 F.3d 1576 (Fed. Cir. 1996), appropriately got rid of experts for claim interpretation, in most cases. The CAFC narrowly defined means plus function claims and caused many lawyers to believe the doctrine of equivalents was practically eliminated, a belief that was further solidified by the decision in *Chuiminatta Concrete Concepts v. Cardinal Indus.,* 145 F.3d 1303 (Fed. Cir. 1998). The court, in *Symbol Techs. Inc. v. Lemelson Med.,* 277 F.3d 1361 (Fed. Cir. 2002), established the doctrine of estoppel in continuation patents, which was a backdoor attack on submarine patents. Congress passed the Digital Millenium Copyright Act, 17 U.S.C. § 1201 et. seq., which prohibits trafficking in technology that is capable of overcoming technological barriers to access copyrighted materials. The

---

2. With all that going on, it's no wonder my hair turned gray. What is particularly disturbing is, I'm only 18.

doctrine of equivalents was apparently resurrected in *Odetics v. Storage Technology Corporation, et al.*, 185 F.3d 1259, (Fed. Cir. 1999) and most important of all, my hair has turned gray.[2]

All of this immediately gives rise to the question; Why did my hair turn gray? The answer to this, and many other fascinating questions, will be forthcoming in subsequent chapters of this book. To begin with, however, I wanted to talk about antitrust law and so that's exactly what I've done.

Section 1

Antitrust Law

1

Antitrust Law

Introduction

When the district court's opinion came down in the Justice Department's case against Microsoft, I sat down to read the entire opinion. Two weeks later I was awakened from my coma and was disappointed to discover that there had been considerable support among my friends, family, and the public-at-large for pulling the plug on the first day. There is a lesson in all this: Never, *ever* try to read that decision. If you are one of those who has actually read the opinion, then you clearly have something fundamentally wrong in your life. For your sake, and the sake of your family, I suggest you follow Buddha's example and go wandering off alone to fast and meditate. It may not help you any, but believe me, you will be providing a valuable service to your family.

In case it isn't perfectly clear by this point, I have absolutely no interest in discussing that case. It is far too esoteric—but more than that, it is BORING.

Since I'm not going to discuss the most publicized antitrust case of this century (note this century is not that old), you're probably wondering why you should continue reading this book. The answer is simple. You paid for it, you may as well read it.

So, what aspect of antitrust law are we going to discuss? We are going to discuss patent and copyright tying.

Patent Tying

Every person who has spent at least five minutes dealing with patent law and/or antitrust law knows that one of the few bright lines in the legal profession is the strict and absolute prohibition on tying the sale of a patented product to the sale of a nonpatented product. This is against public policy, because it involves extension of the patent monopoly beyond that proscribed by Congress. There is a long line of cases supporting that proposition, including *International Salt v. United States,* 332 U.S. 392 (1947); *United States v. Loew's Inc.,* 371 U.S. 38 (1962); *American Tobacco Co. v. United States,* 328 U.S. 781 (1946); *Carter v. Veriflex, Inc.,* 101 F. Supp. 2d 1261, 1267 (C. Dist. Cal. 2000); *Datagate, Inc. v. Hewlett-Packard Co.,* 60 F.3d 1421, 1424 (9th Cir. 1995); *Mallinckrodt v. Medipart,* 976 F.2d 700 (Fed. Cir. 1992); *Monsanto Co. v. Spray-Rite Service Corp.,* 465 U.S. 752 (1984); *Jefferson Parish Hospital District No. 2 v. Hyde,* 466 U.S. 2 (1984); *The Mozart Company v. Mercedes-Benz of North America,* 833 F.2d 1342, 1345 (9th Cir. 1987); *United States v. Aluminum Company of America,* 148 F.2d 416 (2d Cir. N.Y. 1945); *United States v. Grinnell Corp.,* 384 U.S. 563 (1966); *United States Steel Corp. v. Fortner Enterprises,* 429 U.S. 610 (1977); *Universal Analytics, Inc. v. MacNeal-Schwendler Corporation,* 914 F.2d 1256 (9th Cir. 1990); and *White Motor Co. v. United States,* 372 U.S. 368 (1963).

This legal doctrine was last affirmed by the Supreme Court in the case of *Jefferson Parish Hospital District No. 2 v. Hyde,* 466 U.S. 2 (1984). In that case, the Court stated, on page 15:

> For example, if the government has granted the seller a patent or similar monopoly over a product, it is fair to presume that the inability to buy the product elsewhere gives the seller market power. . . . *United States v. Lowes, Inc.,* 371 U.S. 38; 9 L. Ed. 2d 11; 83 S. Ct. 97. Any effort to enlarge the scope of the patent monopoly by using the market power it confers to restrain competition in the markets for a second product will undermine competition on the merits in that second market.

That seems fairly simple and straightforward, and therefore we should be able to move on to another topic. Wrong. In this business nothing is ever sacred, including the doctrine of patent tying. In her concurring opinion in *Jefferson Parish,* my cousin Sandy O'Connor[1] made a statement

---

1. Actually, she's not really my cousin, but she likes to tell people that she is, so who am I to object? I once tried to pull that scam on a federal judge during a conference on

that has been the subject of much commentary. What she said was (pages 34-35):

> [a] common misconception has been that a patent . . . suffice[s] to demonstrate market power . . . [because] a patent holder has no market power in any relevant sense if there are close substitutes for the patented product.

Now, you should know that there are a bunch of people out there who detest the per se patent (and also copyright—which we will discuss later) tying doctrine. The leader of that school was the late Professor Areeda. Now, Professor Areeda, boys and girls, was a member of what is euphemistically referred to as the "Chicago School." It includes such distinguished legal scholars as Judge Robert Bork, who almost made it to the Supreme Court, where he would have been referred to, by me, as "my cousin Bork."

If you are a member of the Chicago School, you believe in three things. First, that Mrs. O'Leary's cow was a socialist bent on destroying the free enterprise system. Second, government should butt out of any and all interference with business, especially in the antitrust area. Third, all antitrust issues, at least as they relate to tying, should require a market analysis of the tying product.

In laymen's terms, what do these things mean? First, Mrs. O'Leary's cow was responsible for the fire that destroyed Chicago. That particular cow had a suspicious past. First, it had been seen to be reading a book written by Eugene V. Debs. Second, there were rumors that it had once worked for the Justice Department's antitrust division. Finally, and most damning of all, the cow was known to be a frequent guest in the home of Theodore Roosevelt.

The part about the free market being left to be the free market is a matter for politicians, and we are not going to touch that subject (or any politicians, for that matter) with a 10-foot pole. Finally, with regard to the market analysis in antitrust law as it relates to tying, that is where the per se patent and copyright tying rules butt heads directly with the Chicago School and like-minded individuals.

---

jury instructions. I told him, "It's funny you should bring that up, your Honor, I was just discussing this with my cousin Sandy last week and she said . . ." The judge: "Your cousin Sandy?" Me: "Why yes, uh, Sandra Day O'Connor." Judge: "I thought O'Connor was her married name." Me (cleverly): "Oops, I guess ya got me." This just goes to prove the old adage that you can fool a federal judge 99 percent of the time, but when you try to pass yourself off as a relative of a Supreme Court Justice, they'll probably nail you.

The essence of a tying case is that it allows a person with market power in the tying product to force purchasers of the tied product to be in a position where they would have to pay noncompetitive (read "higher") prices. Antitrust law frowns upon this practice. The traditional analysis involves a market power analysis of the tying product. This usually involves the messy business of doing an elasticity of demand analysis. Now, elasticity of demand is simply a fancy way of saying that as more competitors come into the market, the price for the accused tying product will go down. If that doesn't happen, then we have inelasticity of demand.

Let's back up for a minute. Before we can really get into the inelasticity/elasticity analysis, we first have to find a relevant market. Actually, these are two sides of the same coin. If I have a 90 percent share of the market for screws, but whenever I try to raise prices people simply start using nails, I'm not able to raise my prices at will because there is elasticity of demand. That is, there is substitutability of product, and people who may want to use my screws are also willing to switch to nails if the price becomes too high.

Since the essence of antitrust law is to promote competition and thereby keep prices competitive (read "low"), elasticity of demand means that even though a person may have a 100 percent share of one product, it does not have monopoly power, because consumers will switch to products that are substitutable. Therefore, the relevant market is the product sold by the accused monopolizer and those products that are easily substitutable for that product.

Obviously the opposite is true in terms of determining that there is inelasticity of demand. If the accused monopolist has a monopoly on screws and when he raises his prices consumers simply pay the higher prices because nails won't suffice for the same purpose, then there is inelasticity of demand and monopoly power in the then-defined market of screws. If the monopolist in the relevant market (screws) now requires purchasers of his screws to also purchase his shoddily constructed screwdrivers, that is a per se violation of the antitrust laws. In other words, it is not necessary to show market power over the screwdrivers; it is the use of the monopoly in screws to force consumers to buy his overpriced and substandard screwdrivers that is a per se violation of the antitrust laws.

That's fine, in theory, but how does it work in practice?

The problem with those types of cases is that a market analysis of the nature required to establish market power in the tying product is extremely difficult, often highly subjective, and, most important, often very expensive. For that reason, relatively few individual plaintiffs pursue those types of cases. More often than not, if a case of that nature is brought, it will be brought by the Justice Department, which has the resources. Often, private companies will piggyback onto the Justice Department's antitrust case so that their lawyers can sit in the courtroom while the Justice Department lawyers present the case, and their lawyers can thereafter tell everybody that they tried an antitrust case. So, let's get back to patent tying.[2]

Now, if you are a member of the Chicago School, and you believe that every antitrust case should be subjected to a strict economic analysis, you are going to have very little, if any, use for an arbitrary bright-line tying test. Obviously, this means hostility to the per se patent tying antitrust theory.

There have been repeated attempts, particularly in the aftermath of *Jefferson Parish,* to amend the antitrust laws by including a requirement that market power in the patented product be established through a market analysis. In other words, there have been numerous attempts in Congress to eliminate the per se patent tying doctrine. One of the more dramatic attempts related to the Patent Misuse Reform Act. The Patent Misuse Reform Act changed the law regarding enforceability of patents. Prior to the Patent Misuse Reform Act, if a patentee was engaged in patent tying, its patent was unenforceable against anyone, even when not affected by the illegal and unlawful patent tying. The Patent Misuse Reform Act amended that law by requiring that, as a prerequisite to asserting the defense of patent misuse (i.e., tying), one had to first establish market power for the patented product in the market in which the patented product competes. That modification to the law was perfectly logical. There is no legitimate reason why a person in competition with the patentee should be able to avail himself of an absolute defense based upon conduct unrelated to the market in which the infringer competes.

An attempt was made to further modify the law by including in the Patent Misuse Reform Act a requirement that, for antitrust purposes, market power must be established in the market in which the tying patented product competes. Those attempts were not successful, and accordingly the Patent Misuse Reform Act does not contain any repeal of the patent tying doctrine.

So, you are probably saying to yourself about now, "I understand it." What you think you understand is that there is a bright-line test for patent tying, and that anyone who has a patented product and ties the sale of that patented product to nonpatented products is a per se violator of the

---

2. For purposes of this discussion, I am separating patent tying from copyright tying. The reason for this is that, with the advent of copyrights on computer software, a new dynamic has arisen that might very well result in a change in the law.

antitrust laws. Well, up until recently I would have said you are absolutely right, that is one of the few bright-line tests in the law and provides the degree of certainty that the law should always provide.

Enter Professor Phillip Areeda. As many of you know, Professor Areeda is generally considered to be the leading authority on antitrust law in this country. Areeda's encyclopedia on antitrust law is an absolute requirement to be in the library of anyone who wishes to practice in this area. Now, as I indicated above, Professor Areeda, being of the Chicago School, does not like and does not believe in the patent per se rule. Accordingly, Professor Areeda came up with a convoluted, and frankly logically absurd, conclusion that per se patent tying doesn't exist. His argument goes something like this:[3] All of the old Supreme Court per se patent tying cases are old and therefore not modern, and therefore can be disregarded. *Jefferson Parish,* which clearly reaffirmed the doctrine of patent tying, was not a patent tying case. It was a market power tying case. Accordingly, everything the majority said about patent tying was just dicta. *Jefferson Parish* went on to hold that, in a market power tying case, one has to prove market power in the market for the tying product or service. This requires a market definition, including geographic definition and analysis regarding elasticity, etc. Since the portion of the Court's decision that reaffirmed the patent tying doctrine was just dicta, it can be disregarded altogether. Therefore, the holding of the Court in *Jefferson Parish* is that, for there to be a tying violation of the antitrust laws, one must go through the economic analysis that the Court required in the *Jefferson Parish* case.

Professor Areeda then couples this with the remarks made by Justice O'Connor and goes on to cite a whole string of non–Supreme Court cases that, according to him, have agreed with Justice O'Connor and held that the mere existence of a patent means absolutely nothing as far as market power is concerned. A reading of those cases reveals that none of them are patent tying cases. Obviously, if one is concerned with market power of the tying product vis-á-vis the products with which it competes, having a patent means nothing. Just because a party has a patent in a particular product doesn't necessarily mean that anyone wants to buy it. That analysis is completely different from the analysis in a patent tying case, where the market power is presumed in the patented product because the patented product, by definition, is unique and useful, and therefore constitutes the entire relevant market. In further support of his position, Pro-

---

3. This is my paraphrasing; if I got this wrong, you can always find that out for yourself by looking up patent tying in Areeda.

fessor Areeda refers to the dissent and the denial of the petition for writ of certiorari in the case of *Data General v. Digidyne Corp.*, 473 U.S. 908 (1985), page 908:

> Drawing distinctions between the permissible and the forbidden in this area is difficult, and the posture of this case—a jury verdict overturned by the District Court but reinstated on appeal—creates an additional layer of complexity, since each court below took a different view of what facts were relevant. Nonetheless, this case raises several substantial questions of antitrust law and policy, including what constitutes forcing power in the absence of a large share of the general market, whether market power over "locked in" customers must be analyzed at the outset of the original decision to purchase, and what effect should be given to the existence of a copyright or other legal monopoly in determining market power.

At stake is more than the resolution of this single controversy or even the clarification of what may seem at times to be a collection of arcane legal distinctions. In the highly competitive, multibillion-dollar-a-year computer industry, bundling of software and hardware, or of operating systems and central processing units, is somewhat common, and any differentiated product is especially attractive to some buyers. The reach of the decision in this case is potentially enormous, and as the United States strongly urges us to do, I would grant certiorari to address the substantial issues of federal law presented

His reasoning is that Justice Blackmun was one of the dissenters in the *Digidyne* certiorari denial, and therefore, even though Justice Blackmun was part of the majority in *Jefferson Parish*, he would probably have changed his mind, if given the opportunity to revisit this issue, and would have sided with Justice O'Connor.

If it appears to you that Professor Areeda reached a conclusion that he wanted and then reasoned backward to find some way to justify his conclusion, you would probably be correct. In fact, that reasoning appears to be so illogical that it is inconceivable that any court could accept it. Right? Wrong.

I am presently up to my eyeballs in this issue. In a recent case, the trial judge had the nerve to grant summary judgment in favor of the defendant and against the plaintiff (my client). The court adopted, almost verbatim, Professor Areeda's analysis, even including his reliance on the dissenting opinion in the denial of the petition for writ of certiorari in

Digidyne, supra. Nobody disputed that there was a patented product and that there were contracts tying the sale of the patented product to the purchase of nonpatented consumables. The court ruled that essentially the per se patent tying rule no longer existed, adopting Areeda's analysis almost verbatim, and then held that because there was no independent economic analysis involving inelasticity of demand and no evidence of relevant geographic market, etc., the plaintiff could not meet its burden in going forward with an antitrust case. The court has certified that case for an appeal and we are presently asking the Court of Appeals for the Federal Circuit (CAFC) to allow the interlocutory appeal.[4] Another incorrect statement by the Court was that at best the patent market power is a rebuttable presumption. No court has ever so held. The presumption is a result of what a patent is. A patent requires that the invention be *unique.*

Copyright Tying

In my mind there is a distinction between patent tying and copyright tying in the area of software copyright tying. In *Digidyne Corp. v. Data General Corp.,* 734 F.2d 1336 (9th Cir. 1984), *cert. denied,* 473 U.S. 908 (1985), the jury had originally found for the plaintiff on software copyright tying. That is, the purchase and use of the defendant's software was conditioned upon the purchase of other products (CPUs). The district court reversed, finding no real market power in the software. The Ninth Circuit reversed the district court's opinion, concluding that there was a presumption of market power because the software was copyrighted, and then further indicating that there was actual evidence of market power. A petition for writ of certiorari was filed with the Supreme Court and was denied. What was of interest, however, was the dissenting opinion as to the denial of the writ of certiorari. This dissenting opinion was written by Blackmun and White. (You may recall that Areeda used Blackmun's dissent as a basis for concluding that if Blackmun had to do *Jefferson Parish* all over again, he would have sided with Justice O'Connor.) The dissent argued that the underlying decision by the Ninth Circuit raised substantial questions about the impact and effect on market power of intellectual properties such as copyrights. It is noteworthy (to me, at least)

---

4. In case you are wondering why the CAFC has jurisdiction, particularly in view of the latest Supreme Court determination that the CAFC does not have jurisdiction over cases where the patent issues are first raised in the counterclaim, the answer is that the original complaint, in addition to alleging patent tying, also sought a declaratory judgment of invalidity of various of the defendant's patents.

that the dissent did not say anything specifically about patent tying. Since patent tying is the area where most of these cases have arisen, one would have expected it to be mentioned if that was also its concern.

Assuming, arguendo, that the concern was for copyright tying rather than patent tying, why should this be?

The answer lies in the nature of software. First, it should be noted that all of the Supreme Court cases confirming the illegality of intellectual property tying occurred before the advent of the personal computer. The fundamental difference between software that is copyrighted and other forms of copyright protection is that software is invisible to the end-user. In this regard, it almost makes no sense to have copyright protection for software, since the whole purpose of copyright law is to protect means of expression and traditionally involved artistic expression, such as books, movies, photographs, etc. The only real protection afforded by software copyright registration is that it prohibits people from purchasing copyrighted software for a limited use, such as one computer only, and then downloading it on multiple computers. As far as the creative process is concerned, however, a software copyright provides very limited protection. The reason for this is that only very limited types of software are copyrightable. Even though one can simply go to the Copyright Office (Library of Congress) and file software, thereby receiving a certificate of registration, that does not mean that the registration is legitimate and/or that everything that is set forth in the copyright registration is copyrightable.

For example, if a particular software program is a direct result of functionality so that anybody seeking to obtain the same function would essentially have to create the same program, that program is not copyrightable. Anyone who knowingly files for a copyright of such software would, in my opinion, subject themselves to the possibility of being sued for fraud on the copyright office in the event they ever attempted to enforce such a copyright registration.

If, on the other hand, there are multiple programs that could be written to accomplish the same result, then a competent programmer, knowing the desired function, would have little or no trouble designing his own program to accomplish those results, thus avoiding copyright protection. This means, in the real world, that if a company were to attempt to sell its non-patented CPUs by tying their sales to the copyrighted software operating system, it would, in reality, have very little market power. Since any competent programmer could devise an operating system for a particular CPU (assuming that the operating system was not written in the only fashion in which it could be to obtain functionality), then anyone who wished to purchase another person's CPU would not be restrained from doing so because of one company's copyrighted operating system. It was probably with these factors in mind that Justices Blackmun and White wrote their dissent regarding the writ of certiorari petition in *Digidyne.*

This is clearly distinct from the situation in patent cases. A patented invention, by definition, is unique and useful. It is the function of the patented invention that matters. This is exactly the opposite of a software copyright registration, wherein pure functionality is the death knoll of a copyright registration.[5]

It should be borne in mind that the petition for certiorari in *Digidyne* was, in fact, denied. Therefore, notwithstanding the views of commentators, and maybe even some lower court decisions, the law of copyright tying, as enunciated in *Jefferson Parish*, remains the law. The ultimate disposal of *Independent Ink* could affect copyright tying as well.

---

5. As those of you familiar with design patents know, this is the same principle that applies to a design patent. If a particular design is necessary for functionality, then the design patent is invalid.

2

Patent and Copyright Misuse, Tortious Interference, Trade Libel, and Other Interesting Stuff

Introduction

The traditional counterclaim in a patent or copyright case is patent or copyright misuse. Generally, this includes an allegation that the patent or copyright registration constituted fraud on the Patent Office (or the Copyright Office of the Library of Congress).

Patent misuse as a result of fraudulently obtained patents occurs more often than one might think. In my experience, these types of cases usually arise in the context of a manufacturer/subcontractor arrangement. They do not normally arise because someone deliberately did not submit prior art to the Patent Office or failed to disclose prior use or experimental results showing that the product doesn't work. Those situations do not often occur because they would require active fraud or gross negligence by the lawyer. Contrary to what many people believe, and contrary to the allegations of inequitable conduct that are routinely filed in patent cases, most patent lawyers have a great deal of integrity and would never intentionally mislead the patent office.[1] In the context of contractor/subcontractor relationships or manufacturer/subcontractor relationships, there is often a belief on the part of one party or the other that, in fact, they

---

1. In addition to being motivated by personal integrity, they're also motivated by the terrible consequences of being caught engaging in such conduct.

13

actually are entitled to claim "inventorship." This can happen, for example, when a manufacturer wants a particular product that will perform a particular function and passes those requirements on to the subcontractor. The subcontractor then makes the device according to the specifications or requirements of the manufacturer. The question then becomes, who actually invented what?

While disputes as to inventorship will often arise between the manufacturer and the subcontractor, they can also arise in situations where the manufacturer, which has applied for and obtained a patent in his or its name, sues a competitor. If the competitor is able to prove that the patent was obtained fraudulently and was being used to establish a monopoly because the patent itself creates market power in the patented product, then the competitor may be able to maintain a counterclaim for violation of the antitrust laws. Even if the counterclaimant is unable to maintain a cause of action for violation of the antitrust laws, because, for example, the counterclaimant cannot establish market power or reasonable likelihood of success in creating a monopoly, it may nonetheless be able to maintain a cause of action on other theories. For example, it may allege tortious interference, unfair competition, or even trade libel for falsely alleging and representing to consumers that the defendant has engaged in willful patent infringement.

The same theories and factors can arise in a copyright infringement case. One caveat regarding market power: In these types of cases, unlike the patent and copyright tying cases, the mere fact that one has a patent or copyright in a particular product does not mean that that person or entity has monopoly power vis-á-vis competitive products. There is often close substitutability between a patented or copyrighted product and other nonpatented or noncopyrighted products. Cases stating that principle are legion.[2]

In a case I presently have pending, there was an interesting trade libel, unfair competition, and tortious interference issue created by virtue of the conduct of the plaintiff. In that case, which is currently pending in the Federal Court in Cleveland, Ohio, the plaintiff, after having filed its lawsuit alleging not only software copyright infringement but a host of other claims of nefarious conduct by my client, proceeded to waive the litigation privilege by disclosing the contents of the complaint

---

2. As indicated above, the mistake made by Professor Areeda, and the court in *Independent Ink*, was that they confused the market power in this type of antitrust case, wherein the issue is the patented or copyrighted products and those that compete with them, versus the market in a tying situation, where the entire relevant market is the patented or copyrighted product.

to the public. People often mistakenly assume that the litigation privilege, which essentially allows the filing of any scurrilous or scandalous pleading one wishes, extends to the ability to publish the allegations in the complaint. In most states, the only allowable publication is to a news media outlet. Many legislatures have determined that it is in the public interest to allow a party to publish allegations in a pleading to a news media outlet, under the theory that if the news media, after investigation, determine that the case is worthy of public attention, they should be allowed to publish the material. In most jurisdictions, however, that is the only allowable publication. In other words, there is a certain irony in the fact that a person may openly publish any allegations he or she wishes but may not thereafter publish those allegations in a different forum.

In this case, the plaintiff took its complaint to a trade show and handed it out to the relatively small number of customers of both the plaintiff and my client, the defendant. In addition, the plaintiff published the allegations in the complaint (as well as the allegations in the motion for preliminary injunction) on the Internet. Because of our firm belief that the allegations were completely untrue and defamatory, we filed a counterclaim for trade libel, defamation, tortious interference, unfair competition, and so on. We have also filed a motion for summary judgment directed against the plaintiff's complaint for copyright infringement, which we should easily be able to win, because, in fact, the source code is quite different. Should we be successful in our motion for summary judgment the only issue going forward would be the issues involved in our counterclaims.

Incidentally, tortious interference, trade libel, and unfair competition are all state law causes of action, which raises two questions. First, if we are successful in throwing out the copyright case, is there any basis for federal jurisdiction, and will this case be transferred to a state court? I have actually seen this occur, particularly where judges were looking for ways to clean their calendar. To avoid that possibility, I always look for a basis for obtaining diversity jurisdiction, which we had in this case. Second, why file for tortious interference as well as unfair competition and trade libel? Tortious interference and trade libel may very well be redundant claims in that both allow for actual as well as punitive damages. Unfair competition, however, often raises (depending upon the state) an entirely different issue, which is double recovery. In many jurisdictions, unfair competition is a matter for the court, not the jury, but it also allows the court to award the wrongdoer's profits, *in addition to* damages. Accordingly, it is always important to allege unfair competition in conjunction with causes of action such as tortious interference, trade libel, etc. Also, false advertising can be alleged. Federal false advertising (under the Lanham Act) carries certain presumptions as to liability. Under federal false advertising, all the plaintiff (or counterplaintiff) must do is show that statements were made that were both false and damaging. The burden then shifts to the defendant to show that the plaintiff was not damaged by virtue of the false representations (although the burden of establishing the amount of such damages always lies with the plaintiff).

This business of making unsupported and unsupportable allegations in a complaint raises an interesting question: At what stage should a plaintiff's discovery be allowed to proceed? In my opinion, the courts should adopt a procedure similar to the preliminary hearing in a criminal case. In other words, a plaintiff should have to establish a prima facie case before being able to proceed with discovery. If a plaintiff, without discovery, cannot even survive a summary judgment motion, the case should be thrown out and sanctions awarded. Too many courts allow a plaintiff to use a complaint as a fishing rod. I believe that lawyers filing such cases should be subject to Rule 11 sanctions.

In another pending software copyright case, I represent a defendant who was sued for copyright infringement. The plaintiff's lawyer registered the software just before suit was filed. This was clearly done for the lawsuit, as the software was created and used many years before filing. The plaintiff moved for a preliminary injunction. The injunction was denied. The court's primary basis for denying the motion was that the software was not subject to copyright protection because the plaintiff's program was nothing more than forms created by others.

In light of the court's decision, my client's then-lawyer should have immediately moved for summary judgment. Instead, all the lawyers set off on a cross-country discovery binge at an enormous cost to my client, a small start-up company. My client's former lawyer also prepared and filed (at considerable expense) an antitrust counterclaim that didn't even contain such important features as a relevant market. After we substituted in, we moved for summary judgment of copyright invalidity and amended the counterclaim so that it was based primarily on a fraudulent copyright registration, which in turn was based on the court's denial of the preliminary injunction motion.[3]

Okay, now let's go do some patent law.

---

3. As you many have surmised, I have a real aversion to excess and inappropriate discovery. A perfect example of this is *Paula Jones v. Bill Clinton*, 57 F. Supp. 2d 719 (E.D. Ark 1999). Jones clearly had no damages, and that was apparent from day one. Eventually former President Clinton was granted summary judgment on that basis alone. The key word is "eventually." Summary judgment should have been sought within the first month. Since Paula Jones couldn't show damages or any discovery that would show damages, the case should have been disposed of immediately. Instead, a lot of irrelevant discovery was allowed, and the result is history.

Section 2

Patents

3

Patents

Patents are probably the most powerful of the intellectual property tools and the ones that give rise to a substantial amount of intellectual property litigation. Fundamentally, a patent is simply a limited monopoly. Accordingly, it very well may be appropriate to think of patents as being a subcategory of antitrust law. In fact, as discussed previously, it is common to see a defense of patent misuse in violation of the antitrust laws as an affirmative defense to a patent infringement case.

The patent monopoly until recently was limited to 17 years' duration for a utility patent and 14 years for a design patent. The new term for a patent is 20 years from the date of filing the application for a utility patent and 14 years from the date of issue for a design patent. The new terms allow us to conform with the rest of the world as part of our ongoing attempts to create international standards in trade (GATT, NAFTA, etc.).[1] Another change has recently been made to bring U.S. law into conformity with international practice in the provision for publication.

By statutory change, 35 U.S.C. 122 (37 C.F.R. § 1.215) now requires publication of pending patent applications. Under the revised law, subject to certain exceptions, all U.S. patent applications filed on or after

---

1. Another potential change in the future is the patent being awarded to the "first to file" as opposed to "first to invent" when two people seek to patent the same invention that they have invented independently. This will avoid expensive and messy interference proceedings in the Patent Office.

November 29, 2000, will be published 18 months after the earliest filing date for which the benefit is being sought. The earliest filing date may be the actual filing date of the application in question or a filing date of an earlier related U.S. or foreign application. The general foundation for this change is to bring the United States law in line with the laws of most foreign countries.

Abandoned applications are not published; neither are provisional, reissue or design applications. However, a published application and its file history contents (to date) are available from the U.S. Patent and Trademark Office (USPTO) upon request. The statute also allows third parties to submit prior art documents deemed to be relevant to patentability within two months of the publication date. Such submissions must be made without comments regarding the relevance.

To avoid publication, an applicant must file an appropriate statement requesting that the application not be published and stating that the application will not be filed in a foreign country that provides for 18-month publication. There is a 45-day grace period for notifying the USPTO of a subsequent foreign filing. Failure to comply results in abandonment of the application. If a patent ultimately issues with claims that are "substantially identical to the claims in the published application," and the patentee has given actual notice of publication to an alleged infringer, the patentee may collect a reasonable royalty for the period between the date of publication and the date of the patent grant. This is similar to the "provisional protection" available in certain European jurisdictions.

A utility patent is one for a device or a method of manufacture, a chemical composition, a drug, or a plant. A person who has obtained a patent has the exclusive right to manufacture, use, and sell the patented device.

In the case of a design patent, the monopoly is directed to the physical appearance of the item that is patented. Design patents are the easiest to obtain, but also, for obvious reasons, they are the easiest to circumvent. All one has to do is make the same product in a different design.

A subtle point with regard to design patents, which often is not understood by inventors, or by lawyers as well, is that if the design is functional rather than merely ornamental, the patent can be invalid for that reason alone. Many times a holder of a design patent, in trying to convince me to take his or her case, has said, "I know I have these infringers right where I want them, because if they try to change the design it won't work." This, of course, is absolutely the last thing that the lawyer who is preparing to file suit on a design patent wants to hear.

This information about design patents is something that can be very useful to general practitioners who may have clients who are all excited about having obtained a design patent and want to know their rights. It is also useful if one has a client who has been accused of infringing a design patent. When defending a design patent case, the first question one asks the inventor in deposition is, "Will this device function equally well if the design is changed?" If the plaintiff is foolish enough to say no, then *you've got him.* Of course, the plaintiff who is represented by competent counsel will say, "Of course you can alter this design; the design has nothing to do with functionality." Isn't it amazing how these cases can turn on such simple and seemingly unimportant points?

Getting back to regular old utility patents: These are much more powerful tools, because hopefully a minor change in the infringing product will not be sufficient to retain the product's commercial value to the infringer.

The main consideration in analyzing patents for infringement, validity, and so on is to recognize that the legal aspect of the patent consists of the claims. If you look at a patent (see appendix), you will see that it consists of many parts. (Incidentally, we will use the term "patent" to indicate utility patents. When referring to design patents, we will call them "design patents.") These parts consist of background of the invention, a brief description of the drawings, an abstract of the invention, a description of the preferred embodiment, and the claims.

Many people (according to recent polls, 72.3 percent of the American public)[2] believe that a patent consists of a description of the invention. They believe that this protects inventors against those who might try to copy their inventions. What most people are thinking of is the description of the preferred embodiment. If this were all the protection afforded by patents, very few patents would be worth anything. The whole idea of the preferred embodiment is just that: an embodiment that is preferred. But this is not the extent of the protection afforded by the patent.

By the same token, another popular misconception (believed by 65.4 percent of the public)[3] is that each and every feature of an invention is covered by a patent. This particular misunderstanding is encouraged by manufacturers who insist on advertising their products as "patented." Most experienced patent lawyers, when they hear that something is advertised as patented, want to know exactly what features are patented before they decide whether to be impressed. Unfortunately, most patent lawyers are easily impressed, even if there is no legitimate reason for it.

One can advertise a car as "patented" when what is patented may be the design of a hubcap. Accordingly, in the technical field of patent law, deciding precisely what is patented and its value, in terms of litigation,

2. I made this up.
3. I made this up too.

will depend on the strength of the patent itself as well as on the breadth of its claims. Ideally for the patent holder, the claims will be broad enough to cover virtually any variation that incorporates the fundamental features and principles of the invention.

For example, if in a preferred embodiment it was disclosed that two panels of a device were fastened by screws and one skilled in the art would realize that they could just as easily be fastened by rivets, then the inventor and his or her lawyer would certainly want to prevent a potential infringer's being able to circumvent the patent by using rivets instead of screws. Accordingly, the claims should probably use language such as "a first panel; a second panel secured to said first panel. . . ." This would obviously cover screws, rivets, nails, glue, cosmic dust, etc.[4]

The other portions of the patent—the background, abstract, and description of the drawings—are fairly self-descriptive. While it is probably not of much concern to those of you who do not write patent applications, a word to the wise to those who do write them: Be careful what goes into the background of the invention and sometimes even into the abstract (although there is a law that the abstract can't be used in interpreting claims), because seemingly innocuous statements that are unnecessary may come back to haunt you. I have seen this happen time and time again. The bottom line is: Don't put anything in a patent that does not have to be there, because it can only be used against you and your client. But be sure you have enough to sustain the patent through all of the attacks that will be made against it.

When a client first appears and says, "I have a great idea and I want it patented," how do you respond? If you are typical of many lawyers, the first thing you will say is, "Great, pay me a big fee and I will see that all of your rights, constitutional and otherwise, are protected." Those lawyers on the other side of the spectrum, who never commit themselves to anybody at any time, anywhere, because they are afraid they'll get in trouble, will say something along the lines of "That's great, but there is nothing I can do for you, I only do divorce work. Say, I don't suppose you would like to get a divorce?"

Then, of course, there are those of us in the middle of the road who really want to help this poor fellow (or woman or corporation), if it's appropriate.[5] For those middle-of-the-roaders, the first question that should be asked is, "When you say that you have a great idea, does this mean

---

4. This is a simplistic example, but this is supposed to be a simplistic book. If we wanted to write a complicated book we would use a complicated example.

5. The word "appropriate" is a technical term in patent law relating to the number of billable hours needed to pay the rent.

you actually have an invention, or does it mean that you just have an idea?"

The distinction is important. One of the great common fallacies of 20th-century America (now a great fallacy of 21st-century America) is that one can obtain a patent for a mere idea. Many people think this means a way of doing business, a way of cheating your neighbor, a way of doing household chores, etc. The most common fallacy is that there is protection for someone's *idea* for an invention.

A former law school colleague of mine (who will remain nameless because I don't remember his name), on discovering that I had actually taken a job as a patent lawyer, informed me that his mother had come up with a great idea. Because I suspected that anyone who had raised this particular individual would have a difficult time coming up with any great ideas, I was somewhat skeptical. As it turned out, my skepticism was more than justified. On observing the abundance of hair left scattered on the floor of most barbershops and beauty parlors, this guy's mother had concluded that someone should invent a commercial use for all that hair. He then wanted to know how much it would cost his mother to have this idea patented. As it turned out, not only was the idea a bad idea, but the thousand-dollar check he gave me to protect it *bounced.*

Not a week later I received a call from another of my classmates, who informed me that her mother had come up with an equally great invention: paper underwear. It was then that I made the decision never to attend another class reunion for my old law school. Fortunately, they have scheduled only one class reunion in the entire 34 years since graduation, and that had to be canceled because even the organizers weren't going to attend.

So what is the point of all this complaining and wondering and meandering into experiences of the past? The point is, a patent has to be on an invention, not an idea. The saying used in patent law is, "If you can't build it, you ain't invented it." So, the first thing you tell this budding would-be entrepreneur and inventor extraordinaire is that he or she must actually have produced something tangible. This does not mean that the inventor must actually have made the physical article, but at least he or she must have a diagram, or a schematic, or a specific set of instructions, or something showing how the thing can be made.

The next question you have to ask, and this is extremely important, is, "Have you ever shown this invention *to anyone at any time* before you came in here?" You will be surprised how many people have shown their invention around or actually used it, or have had friends use it, or maybe even have sold it or offered to sell it before coming to see you. The most common example of this is people displaying their inventions at trade shows. Trade shows are the bane of every patent lawyer's existence.

The reason for this concern is, if an invention has been used or sold in the United States, or advertised or published anywhere on the planet, that person has one year from that date within which to file the patent application in the United States Patent Office or lose the patent rights altogether. This may even apply to an offer to sell before the product was ever built. I recently lost a case (oh, how I hate that) where sales were made *to the inventor* by a supplier. This created a one-year bar (*Special Devices, Inc. v. OEA, Inc.*, 270 F.3d 1353 (Fed. Cir. 2001)). This was a case of first impression.

This rule, which I refer to as the U.S. rule, is among the most liberal in the world. Most countries require a filing of the patent application before any public use or disclosure. It is extremely important that a lawyer dealing with a potential inventor understand both the one-year U.S. rule and the no-prior-disclosure foreign rules. Many inventions are manufactured and/or sold abroad, and many inventors do not think of this until after they have already lost their patent rights by public use or sale before they file for patent protection. If an inventor comes to you and says, "I am planning on showing my device at next week's trade show," you'd better tell her that that may cause a complete waiver of patent rights in many foreign countries and that she has set the clock in motion for filing a U.S. application within one year. While I said that this is the second question you should ask, it is actually the first question you should ask, because if that person leaves your office and then does something that causes a waiver of her future patent rights and you have not informed her of the dangers, guess who is going to be held responsible? I suggest that you not only make these disclosures but that you document in writing that you have made these disclosures and that the inventor has fully understood what the risks are and what the obligations are in terms of the U.S. and foreign patent laws. If you are hiring a patent lawyer, make sure that the lawyer has all these procedures firmly in place.

The next question you have to ask is, did this person actually invent the device he is bringing me? While the answer seems obvious, you would be amazed (or maybe you wouldn't) at how many people think that they can get a patent on somebody else's invention if they are the first to think of patenting it. I have found this to be true particularly with regard to foreign inventions. For some reason, there are people out there (they probably have their own clubs and wear matching T-shirts) who believe that if they can bring a foreign invention into this country, they have the right to obtain the U.S. patent rights. Guess what? They are wrong. Only the inventor can obtain a patent. This is true, incidentally, even if the inventor works for a company and the company has all of the patent rights. The patent will not issue in the name of the company, although the company may very well be listed as an assignee of the patent. The patent must issue in the name of the inventor, and the inventor must sign the disclosure. (There are exceptions to the signing rule in the event that a previous employee, for example, refuses to sign off on an application when he or she is clearly obligated to do so.) As a general rule, however, the inventor must sign, and the patent will issue only to the inventor or inventors. Occasionally one runs into a situation where a person is a co-inventor and wants to be listed as the sole inventor. This is not allowed.

I actually encountered one situation where the sole inventor had listed another individual as a co-inventor because that second individual was a business partner and a financial contributor, and the inventor felt that it would be a nice gesture to include this person as a co-inventor. Those individuals subsequently had a major falling out and decided to go their separate ways. Suddenly, the true inventor woke up and found that the co-inventor was making, using, and selling the device in competition with the inventor. The lawyer who had handled the matter readily acknowledged that the so-called co-inventor was not actually an inventor and that the lawyer knew it at the time. Nonetheless, he had acceded to the wishes of both of these parties, and, of course, he later regretted that decision. In case it is not fairly obvious, the inventor, and only the inventor, has a right to be listed on the patent.

So now you have established certain basic facts from your interview. First, the inventor is the actual inventor; second, he actually has an invention; and third, he has not been using, making or selling his invention for more than one year before he came to see you. Does this mean you can go ahead and file a patent application? Not unless you are a patent lawyer. Only a patent lawyer, or patent agent, can represent people in front of the U.S. Patent Office. Now, if you are a patent lawyer and are reading this book, the big question is, why? Can't you find something better to do with your time? If you can't, then you should probably not be writing patent applications anyway. But enough of this—let's get back to the client.

Now that we have established that this client has a legal right to file for a patent application and you are still advising him whether he should go forward and file a patent (that is, whether you should refer him to your friend Joe, down the corridor, who actually is a licensed patent lawyer but is hurting for clients), you might want to make some further inquiries, or at least give him some helpful hints. The first hint you might wish to pass his way is that if someone else has invented this same device and has actually patented it, he can forget it. Also, if someone else has actually invented this device and it is out in some printed publication or in public use in the United States, and that person invented before he did, he can also forget it.

As indicated above, in the United States we have what is called the "first-to-invent rule." Many other countries have the first-to-file rule. There is a movement afoot (isn't there always?) to change the rule in the United States to first-to-file as well. The advantage of the first-to-file rule is that it is pretty simple, not to mention it is in conformity with the rest of the world. As it stands now, however, we still have the first-to-invent rule, and this is a major source of contention in many patent suits. If a new client sitting in front of you was actually the first to invent, then she may be okay, except for two other possible scenarios. The first scenario is that she was the first to invent but sat on her rights, and in the meantime, someone else in the United States made, used, or sold her invention more than one year before she filed her application.

I had a case following precisely this scenario involving kaleidoscopes, *Beachcombers v. Wildwood Creative Products*, 31 F.3d 1154 (Fed. Cir. 1994), in which the inventor claimed to have invented his device many years before he filed his patent application and basically sat on his rights because he was short of money or some such reason. Now, there is another doctrine, known as "abandonment," which says that if you sit on your rights you may lose them.

The problem with abandonment as a defense is that it becomes a subjective issue. There are no hard-and-fast rules, as there are in issues such as first to invent, prior public disclosure, etc. Whether a person abandoned an application or not is often decided simply on the visceral response of the trier of fact. It is actually an estoppel type of defense, in that the person asserting it usually claims that during the period between invention and the filing of the patent, the accused has, not knowing about the invention, embarked on the making, selling, obtaining customers, marketing, etc., of the subsequently patented product. In the *Wildwood* case, the abandonment defense was the only defense that did not succeed. We started this discussion, however, not on the abandonment defense but on the issue of first to invent.

In the *Wildwood* case, another person had invented, but not patented, the identical kaleidoscope that the patentee was asserting against my client. One of the issues in the case then became the question of who was the first to invent: the patentee, who was suing my client, or this other individual, who had never filed for a patent? The patentee had filed his patent application subsequent to the invention date of this third party. Accordingly, there was a presumption that the third party had actually invented it first. This presumption was rebuttable, however, and that's when we got into this question of when the inventor actually invented his device. The inventor produced some notebook pages and testimony that indicated he had actually invented this device many, many years before he had filed his application, and also many, many years before the third party had invented the identical device. It was because of his long delay from the time of actual invention until the time of his filing for a patent application that we raised the unsuccessful defense of abandonment.

So we raised another defense: prior public use. If the invention is in prior public use or sale more than a year before the actual filing date of the patent application, this invalidates the patent. In this particular case, the third party had displayed her identical kaleidoscope at a party approximately one year and one month before the filing date of the application, and accordingly, the jury found the patent to be invalid.

This is the danger of sitting on one's rights. Had the inventor filed his patent application two months earlier, he would have been able to withstand this defense and his patent would probably be in existence today. In addition, he probably would have won the case, because my client's product read directly on the claims of the patent that were anticipated by the third party's prior art. In other words, the applicable claim of the plaintiff's patent, the prior art device, and my client's device were all identical as far as the relevant features were concerned. My client's device, because it was invented and sold after the issuance of the patent, would have been an infringing product but for the fact that the third party's identical product was invented, used, and publicly disclosed more than a year before the filing of the application that eventually ripened into the patent asserted against my client. In patent law, as in life, timing is everything.

4

Discovery

As I stated previously, nothing is more aggravating in patent infringement cases than discovery. Even legitimate discovery is aggravating. Unfortunately, in this particular field of law, there are endless opportunities for abuse of the discovery process, and it sometimes seems as though every patent lawyer in the country has taken special graduate courses on how to abuse discovery (the author, of course, being the sole and glowing exception to this rule). If you are not actually involved in patent infringement litigation, you probably will not be involved in the annoying conduct of those who are. Nonetheless, if you are representing clients who may be involved in patent litigation and are coming to you for advice, you want to be able to forewarn them in a reasonably intelligent fashion as to what they might be facing.

An issue in virtually every patent infringement case is the validity of the patent. Even though a patent has been issued by the United States Patent Office, the question of whether that patent should ever have issued is one that can be addressed de novo in the trial court. One of the reasons for this is that patent prosecution is ex parte where there is no opportunity for anyone opposing the patent to be heard.[1] (This is not

---

1. Contrary to popular belief, the term "patent prosecution" does not mean criminal prosecution of patent lawyers, although many people strongly advocate such prosecution. It actually means the process of shepherding a patent application through the Patent Office until it ripens into the golden fruit of an actual patent with a neat blue ribbon.

the case in all countries. For example, in Japan, a patent application must be published before it is issued.) As it stands today, however, all proceedings involving the initial issuance of a patent are ex parte, and therefore it is appropriate to allow a patent to be attacked de novo in a federal proceeding in which an opposing party can bring to the attention of the court prior art, as well as arguments that may not have been considered by the patent examiner.[2]

In point of actual fact, patent examiners are overworked and have very little opportunity to analyze prior art properly in deciding whether to issue a patent. Also, as a practical matter, the Patent Office often considers only prior art patents that are contained within the Patent Office. As a result, patent examiners seldom have the opportunity to consider publications that are not referred to in patents as well as actual devices sold, etc.

A lawyer representing a party accused of patent infringement will want to do everything within her power to uncover any prior art that might have prevented the patent from issuing in the first instance. Accordingly, for those who can afford it, this often involves running around the world on a wild-goose chase, or sometimes even a tame-goose chase, digging up publications, papers, articles, advertisements, brochures, sales invoices, and the like. It also involves taking the depositions of everyone who ever had anything to do with the invention, as well as anyone in the field of the invention in this country or foreign countries, to find out if there is any prior art of which they may be aware. Usually, courts will respond favorably to requests to keep a lid on this kind of discovery (and there are statutory limits as well) because it can very easily get out of hand, and the costs can be astronomical. Incidentally, costs are always a major factor in patent infringement litigation, because one or the other of the parties often is a well-established commercial entity and may attempt to use its power of the pocketbook to make the litigation so costly that the other side will be forced into a settlement.

One example of discovery run amuck occurred in a case that we tried recently (*Automotive Products, PLC v. Tilton Engineering, Inc.,* 33 U.S.P.Q. 2d 1065 (C. Dist. Cal. 1995). In that case, there was an issue of prior public use. As discussed earlier, if a product has been used more than a year before the filing of the patent application, the patent may not issue. There is a question in many cases as to what actually constitutes prior public use. Public use, for example, has been

---

2. Subject to the new patent provisions allowing publication prior to issuance, as discussed previously.

held to exist where someone utilized an invention in a commercial device, even though the public was never aware of the existence of the device or its use. On the other hand, public use has been held not to be prior public use for purposes of this statute if the use was experimental. This is true even when the experimental use is continued for a period of years, as in the case of *City of Elizabeth v. The American Nicholson Pavement Co.*, 97 U.S. (7 Otto) 126 (1877), which involved wooden pavement for roads.

In the *Tilton* case, our client, Tilton Engineering, had developed a so-called carbon/carbon clutch for use in racing cars. Before deciding whether it had invented a commercially viable product, Tilton had to test it. The only way you can properly test automobile racing components is to use them in real races. Accordingly, Tilton contacted a number of racing teams and asked them if they would be willing to test these clutches in an actual race situation. All of the teams did so, and did so quite successfully. In fact, the U.S. Grand Prix in Detroit was won by a team using a Tilton clutch. The winning car was driven by the late great Brazilian race car driver, Ayrton Senna. That, incidentally, was the first time in more than 20 years that a race had been won by a team using a clutch that was not manufactured by Automotive Products, Tilton's adversary in the litigation.

Automotive Products decided to depose every single race team that ever used the Tilton clutch. This resulted in extensive discovery all over the country that was extremely expensive to our client. (We later filed antitrust counterclaims, which resulted in more hopping around the country chasing information that Automotive Products thought might be useful in its case.)

In addition to discovery related to chasing elusive prior art, the discovery of the parties themselves can often be extremely burdensome and can involve multiple discovery issues. It is not at all uncommon to utilize a referee during depositions because of the constant haggling that goes on in these cases. (Some of the haggling is appropriate and unavoidable, but much of it simply stems from the particular personality quirks one finds in engineers and others of us with technical backgrounds who believe in excruciating attention to detail, even when it is not appropriate.)

The first thing a defendant in one of these cases will do is demand every piece of paper ever written by any employee of the plaintiff who had anything to do with the patent, with any products made in accordance with the teachings of the patent, with any discussions concerning products even remotely related to the patented product, and so on. You also can expect that the lawyer who prepared the patent application will be deposed, and there will be numerous attempts to obtain all of his or her documents, including drafts of patent applications, correspondence with the inventor, correspondence with the principals of the corporation, and so on.

One reason there is such extensive discovery of the principals of the corporation as well as the inventors is because, unfortunately, in virtually every one of these cases there is a momentous undertaking to attempt to find fraud on the Patent Office. The technical term now is "inequitable conduct," but it still amounts to fraud, which means willful misrepresentations that are material and that are made to the Patent Office during the prosecution of the patent.

Accordingly, attempts will be made to find out if there was any prior art known to the principals of the company or the inventors or the lawyers that was not disclosed to the Patent Office. There will be concerted efforts to depose the inventor to find out what each and every word, sentence, and paragraph in the patent means. This is an area ripe for this kind of discovery because in the real world, what often happens is that a disclosure comes from someone in the research and development (R & D) department, which then goes to the in-house patent department, which in turn forwards it to an outside patent counsel. The outside patent counsel then sits down and writes a patent application based pretty much on the information obtained from either the in-house patent counsel or the personnel in R & D.

Often patent applications are written by lawyers based on their understanding of the art and without a careful ongoing working relationship with the inventor or inventors. Once a patent lawyer has prepared the application and submitted it to the inventor, the inventor often will simply sign the documents without reading them carefully, assuming the lawyer probably got it right. The technical person who is the inventor simply may read the material to determine whether it accurately describes the invention. In reality, patents will contain a lot of additional information, such as why the product was needed in the first place, what problem the invention solves, and why and how it solves the problem. The subtleties of what is actually contained in the patent itself are very seldom understood by the inventor and, quite frankly, are very seldom fully understood by the lawyer who writes the application. One reason is that often those who write patent applications are not those who litigate them. A litigator fully understands that a patent is nothing more than a trial exhibit and, therefore, should be carefully reviewed with an eye toward how it is going to resonate in front of a judge or jury.

Litigating lawyers are often fully aware that there is a failure of communication between the inventor and the lawyer, and they will subject the inventor or inventors to an excruciatingly exact questioning about what is contained in the patent. I had a case recently where the inventor (who was dyslexic) was subjected to almost seven full days of cross-examination in deposition of a simple four-page patent. (Federal rules now limit depositions to seven hours—Thank you, Creator!) Unfortunately, the inventor and the lawyer who wrote the patent had not been in careful communication, and the inventor's deposition resulted in a number of seeming contradictions of what was contained in the four corners of the patent itself.

As is often the case in litigation, however, a perceived gain actually may be a loss. In that particular case, the lawyers for the defendant thought they had achieved a great deal in the deposition. They then proceeded to subject the inventor to excruciatingly painful cross-examination at trial. In doing so, they forgot one of the cardinal rules of jury trial litigation: Don't antagonize the jury and make them feel sorry for the person being cross-examined. (That is a little cardinal rule I made up myself, but if you think about it, it makes sense.) Accordingly, in closing argument I was able to point out the fact that these people were not trying to defend the case on the merits but were trying to take advantage of an inventor who was dyslexic and who was obviously quite honest in answering the questions that were put to him. As I was delivering this exquisitely sensitive and emotionally draining closing argument, I noticed that almost every one of the jurors nodded in agreement (no, they weren't dozing off) when I started talking about the unfairness of the cross-examination. To no one's surprise (except probably opposing counsel's), the jury came back quite quickly with a verdict in our favor. The truth of the matter was, we deserved to win, and the insignificant mistakes in cross-examination that were made by the inventor were, quite frankly, just that—insignificant. Lawyers sometimes lose perspective and think that any contradiction they can find is a great breakthrough. Jurors usually use common sense and do a pretty good job of focusing on the real issues.

These more esoteric, detailed discussions are probably more appropriate for a patent lawyer, but if you are advising clients, it certainly will make you appear much smarter in their eyes if you can explain to them what they might be facing in terms of all the little ramifications of this kind of litigation.

5

Attorney-Client Privilege

This is perhaps one of the most troubling and unsettled areas of patent infringement litigation.

Suppose a client comes to you and says, "Listen, I have this new product line, and the future of my company depends on it. We have already gone into production, and we have sales orders out the wazoo [that's a technical Latin term that I won't go into right now]. Yesterday, someone in our office discovered that there is a patent that issued last week, and it looks like it might cover our new product." Of course, your first response is, "Hey, I'll send this to my friend Joe down the hall who is a patent lawyer, and we'll get his opinion." Now the first question is, is that the right thing to do? The answer probably is yes. One reason the answer is yes is that if it comes out that your client was aware of the existence of the patent and did not seek legal advice before going forward with the product, the jury can consider that factor in determining whether the infringement was willful, which can result in treble damages.

Now you have another problem. Joe calls you up the next day and says, "Hey, I've looked over this patent and I've looked over your client's product, and I think your client probably infringes." So you say, "Joe, send me a letter and tell me how my client infringes." Right or wrong? Well, it's a dilemma. The first dilemma is, what if Joe's wrong? Do you want your client's company to be stuck with a letter in your files or its files stating that its product infringes when, in fact, it doesn't infringe?

On the other hand, what if Joe's right? Do you tell your client to go ahead anyway if your client says she's not sure whether the other person intends to enforce his patent?

There is an additional question involved in all of these cases: Even if the patent is infringed, is the patent valid? Remember, we are not just talking about whether a patent is valid or infringed but whether specific claims are valid and infringed. You can have a patent in which certain claims are valid and other claims are invalid, and in which certain claims may be infringed and other claims not infringed by the same product.

What do you do? The first rule of thumb is, don't ever get an opinion in writing that is contrary to your client's position. Some may disagree with this advice. Some people may believe there is an ethical obligation to obtain a written opinion from every lawyer who looks at your client's case and gives an evaluation, whether that evaluation is helpful or harmful. I know of no rule of ethics that requires this, and I do not believe it is something that needs to be done. I have had more unnecessary problems caused by off-the-cuff written opinions by lawyers that were very harmful to my clients' positions and that were totally unnecessary and absolutely wrong. (This includes memos to the file. Never write a memo to the file.) I personally will never give a written opinion to a client that may someday find its way into evidence and be harmful to the client's position.

This is something of which the general practitioner, who is advising a client in patent matters, should be acutely aware. This business of writing gratuitous harmful opinions is unfortunately all too common among intellectual property lawyers who do not try cases and who are not aware of the significance of what they are doing. Accordingly, when you send an issue of potential infringement by your client for evaluation by another lawyer, tell that lawyer to be sure to contact you with his or her oral opinion before putting anything in writing. Even if the lawyer has an opinion favorable to your position, you still do not necessarily want to obtain it in writing. All of these writings may prove to be discoverable, and you want to be sure that an opinion favorable to your side is one that will withstand scrutiny under cross-examination in court. The lawyer who writes an opinion concerning validity and infringement also should be aware of the fact that he or she will probably be "witness number one" in any patent infringement case.

The reason the lawyer's opinion will probably find its way into evidence is that on the issue of willfulness, where a client is accused of willfully infringing the patent, that client is going to want to be able to rely on advice of counsel. Accordingly, that client will have letters from a lawyer indicating it has a right to make, use, or sell the accused infringing product. Once that letter has been introduced into evidence, the privilege is waived, and any opinions concerning validity and infringement of the accused product and the patent in suit may be discoverable and can be used in evidence. Also, material that may have contributed to the lawyer's opinion may be discoverable, including matters in other cases involving the same parties and/or similar technologies.

In my opinion, the best way to approach this problem is to retain the services of a patent litigator in whom you have complete confidence. (Fat chance.) That litigator should in turn contact one or more lawyers to obtain validity and infringement opinions. Of course, the litigating lawyer should give you her first impression and opinion. If she tells you that your client is in serious trouble and jeopardy, then you should seriously consider negotiations. If she tells you that in her opinion the patent is either invalid or non-infringing or both, then you should suggest to her that she obtain written advice from other non-litigation patent lawyers that would reflect her opinions. In other words, the first analysis should be done by a litigating attorney, and you should consult with her. These consultations will, of course, be confidential. (One hopes. Nothing should be taken for granted in an area where you know you may be waiving privilege.)

The attorney-client privilege concerns extend beyond opinions on infringement and validity. For example, the attorney-client privilege may be waived if a client conveys to a third party the lawyer's opinion relating to validity and infringement of a patent.

In other words, attorney-client privilege can be waived in a number of ways in patent infringement litigation; therefore, parties and lawyers should be extremely careful in all of their correspondence. Everything that is written should be written with an eye to the fact that it may some-day find itself as evidence in litigation. A letter from a client to a third party discussing a lawyer's opinion about infringement litigation may open a door to other correspondence between the lawyer and the client that also relates to infringement and validity. It may open the door to such correspondence even if the correspondence was written after the client wrote to the third party discussing the lawyer's opinions that pre-dated the subsequent opinions from other lawyers.

I cannot overemphasize the importance of extreme care in all attorney-client correspondence and all correspondence from a client to any other person that refers to a lawyer's opinions. It is amazing the kinds of trouble that can be created when people do not consider the ultimate repercussions of their conduct, and particularly when they do not consider that their conduct may someday find its way into evidence in court. More than a few lawyers have found themselves pulled into litigation as witnesses because of some ill-considered opinions or off-the-cuff letters that they wrote to clients. Clients should be cautioned never to discuss their lawyer's opinions with anyone under any circumstances at any time. If a client is going to express an opinion or take a position based on his lawyer's advice, he should be extremely careful not to state that he is relying on opinions of lawyers and should not indicate in his correspondence what those lawyers' opinions are.

Another example of attorney-client discoverable material in patent infringement cases may be information given by a client to a lawyer or correspondence from a lawyer to a client as it relates to other inventions and other patents that are not even the patents in suit. Once again, great care should be exercised in all correspondence between lawyer and client. Also along these lines, the files of a lawyer prosecuting a patent involved in the litigation, or even patents held by a party who is being sued, may become open books to opposing sides. Lawyers should be very careful about keeping notes to themselves, particularly when those notes may reflect badly on their clients.

On some occasions, lawyers have even prepared drafts of declarations for their clients' signatures without conferring with their clients first to determine if the contents were correct. I had a case where the contents of drafts of declarations, which were never shown to or discussed with the client, were obtained by another party in discovery and then used as evidence in proceedings involving inequitable conduct.

A general rule of thumb in patent cases (and in other cases as well, for that matter) is that lawyers should never prepare documents and keep them in a file when those documents might someday be used adversely to their clients. Clients should never assume that correspondence between them and their lawyers as it relates to patents and particularly as it relates to the patents of third parties will be maintained in confidence.

Unfortunately, this area of attorney-client privilege is one that is not well defined, and the law seems to be made on a case-by-case basis. General practitioners such as you (if you are reading this book) probably have clients who are involved heavily in intellectual property matters and who may not as yet have obtained the services of a patent lawyer. Even if they have obtained the services of patent lawyers, their patent lawyers' expertise may be limited to the writing of patent documents, and those lawyers may not be sensitive to the litigation repercussions of papers that they prepare. Accordingly, the general practice lawyer or in-house counsel who represents a client involved in the research and development and protection of intellectual property rights should review very carefully all the matters between the client and the patent lawyer who is handling her affairs, as well as be very careful when advising the client about what kinds of notes and records she should maintain and what kinds of correspondence she should have between herself and her lawyer.

6

Notes and Records

Research and Development

Since a primary concern in most patent infringement cases is the data of development and reduction to practice, it is extremely important to advise your clients that they maintain detailed notes and records of all of their scientific developments. This is an area in which many people fall down. There is nothing worse than having to try to recapitulate research and development and reduction to practice of an invention when the notes are sporadic, illegible, and contradictory. Accordingly, you should advise your clients to have special forms prepared that they maintain at their workstations, and all research and development (R & D) people should very carefully document everything they do. Of course, these forms are discoverable; therefore, such forms should be prepared with an eye toward the fact that they may be reviewed someday by an aggressive opponent in a patent litigation or intellectual property lawsuit.

The bottom line is that many problems that arise in patent infringement litigation are totally unnecessary and could have been prevented by attention to the process by the inventors, by corporate counsel, by patent counsel, and by corporate executives. It is so frustrating to be involved in patent litigation where, for example, you have a perfectly good and valid patent and an open and obvious infringer and yet find yourself unable to enforce the patent because of trivial and unnecessary mistakes made in the prosecution, because of letters written that were not carefully considered, or because of any number of reasons that involve people not thinking in terms of litigation but thinking simply in terms of getting a patent or meeting some corporate or business objective.

For this reason, there should be careful consultation not only with patent prosecution lawyers and corporate lawyers but also with patent litigation lawyers throughout every stage of every element of R & D undertaken by any entity serious about protecting and enforcing its rights. I cannot state this too strongly.

Remember, in attempting to enforce a patent, it will almost always be necessary to rely on corporate records in terms of R & D, reduction to practice, and so on. All of these records are discoverable, and your opponent will discover all of the bad as well as the good.

On the other side, if you are defending against a patent, you should fully explore all available discovery avenues and make sure you find all of the other side's warts and missteps along the way.

It is unfortunate, in my opinion, that so many of these cases involve turning over every rock to find out which bugs can be located thereunder, instead of dealing with the merits of the cases. Unfortunately, this is the state of affairs in patent litigation, and those who do not adequately prepare for potential litigation every step of the way can expect trouble.

Sales, Advertising, and Marketing

Records relating to sales and advertisement of an accused product may be fair game. To some extent it depends upon the judge. Some judges require production of all financial records, including all sales invoices, whereas other courts are far more lenient and require only the production of summaries.

One problem that often arises is the determination of profits. This is a concern that arises not only in patent infringement litigation but also in antitrust litigation and virtually any areas of corporate litigation involving disputes over a person's rights to sell and commercially utilize intellectual property.

At one time, I represented a Fortune 500 company that did not maintain profit records by item. It maintained its records regarding profits by division and lumped all of its items into a specific division. This particular company was a foreign corporation, and there was a great deal of agitation with the other side seeking to establish a profit margin on the particular accused item. (This was not actually a patent infringement case; it was an antitrust action. Nevertheless, the problem is the same kind of problem that often arises in patent litigation.

Any litigation involving an attempt by one side or the other to establish profits as opposed to mere gross income is inevitably going to involve accounting problems and, thus, accountants pawing through corporate records. Accordingly, a lawyer whose client is likely to become involved in intellectual property litigation on whatever side of the issue (often parties will find themselves both plaintiffs and counterdefendants or defendants and counterplaintiffs in the same action) should bear in mind that the accounting records may very well be fair game for opposing counsel, or, in the alternative, you may find that your client may wish to use its own accounting records.

In the case of large corporations, the accounting records usually are maintained in a pretty careful fashion. Small companies, however, are notorious for maintaining bad financial records. While many lawyers do not feel that the financial records of their clients are of concern, I would recommend that you have a heart-to-heart with your corporate clients or, if you are in-house counsel, with your accounting department to make sure that your records will be letter-perfect for presentation to a judge or jury. (This is kind of like the theory of wearing clean underwear in case you're involved in an automobile accident. Ask your mother if you don't know what I'm talking about.) Always assume that someday all of your client's records will see the light of day, and you want to make sure that when they do, they are seen in the light most favorable to your client and in a manner most easily understood by the trier of fact. (I am not one of those who believe that confusion is an appropriate tactic, and I have never known it to be successful. Juries can spot you and they hate you for it.)

Another area ripe for discovery is advertising. Because patent infringement arises not only from making but also from selling, your client's marketing plans, including internal memos and correspondence with advertising agencies, may be discoverable. The danger this creates is that marketing departments are notorious for bragging about their successes in monopolizing particular products. I have sometimes shuddered at the material I have found within the folders of marketing vice-presidents. Marketing plans and tracing of results can often cause a simple patent infringement case to suddenly become a major antitrust case.

The *Tilton* case, which I referred to previously, was commenced by Automotive Products as a declaratory judgment action to have the Tilton patent declared invalid. Tilton counterclaimed for patent infringement, and we thereafter began our own discovery. In the course of that discovery we obtained Automotive Products' marketing documents, and in those marketing documents we discovered memos that subsequently became the foundation for an antitrust case. The result of that case was that Tilton obtained more than $20 million from a case that was not even instituted by it in the first place.

Accordingly, if you represent a client that has intellectual property and is involved in the marketing of that intellectual property, you should make it a point to go through the documents contained within its marketing department carefully, and, more important, you should have ongoing seminars and communications with the marketing department so that it does not generate documents that can come back to haunt it at a later date. This is particularly important when working as in-house counsel for large corporations that have large and often hyperactive marketing departments that view their own success by how successful they are in getting rid of unwanted competition.

Conclusion

As shown by the last several chapters, the areas about which you need to be very concerned, whether acting as a plaintiff or defendant, corporate counsel, or counsel for corporations that may become involved in intellectual property litigation, are the following:

1. All documents relating to research and development;
2. All attorney-client communications concerning research and development, marketing, and discussions about your client's patents and third party's patents as well;
3. Sales and accounting records; and
4. Marketing documents.

Once again, please bear in mind that most, if not all, litigation problems in intellectual property and patent law in particular can be avoided by always thinking in terms of potential litigation.

7

Court Versus Jury: Who Decides What

Obviousness and Anticipation

In the Court of Appeals for the Federal Circuit (CAFC) decision, *Hilton Davis Chemical Co. v. Warner-Jenkinson Co.*, 62 F.3d 1512 (Fed. Cir. 1995), later decided by the Supreme Court, Judge Nies in a dissenting opinion stated:

> In addition to the requirement of distinct claims, the Act of 1870 changed the way patent cases were thereafter tried. *Jury trials virtually disappeared, not to be seen again in any numbers for over a century,* indeed, until the creation of this court. *n19* Prior to the 1870 Act, a patentee had to sue in equity for an injunction where monetary relief was in the form of an accounting for an infringer's profits. To obtain "damages" for the patentee's own losses, the patentee also had to sue at law. The 1870 Act gave equity courts in patent infringement suits the special power to award common law damages. See *Root v. Railway Co.,* 105 U.S. (15 Otto) 189, 205-07, 26 L. Ed. 975 (1881). Since most patentees wanted an injunction available only in equity, as well as the equity discovery procedure to aid in proof of infringement, the equity court became the forum of choice.
>
> *n19* In *Blonder-Tongue Lab. v. Univ. of Illinois Found.,* 402 U.S. 313, 336 n.30, 28 L. Ed. 2d 788, 91 S. Ct. 1434 (1971), the Su-

preme Court noted that *in the three-year period spanning 1968-1970, only 13 of 382 patent cases going to trial were jury trials. In contrast, fiscal years 1992-1994 saw 163 of 274 patent trials being tried to a jury.* See *Lockwood*, 50 F.3d at 980, 33 U.S.P.Q.2d at 1908. (emphasis added)

As was correctly pointed out by Judge Nies, the utilization of juries in patent infringement cases is a relatively new development. As a result of that new development, there has been some confusion about the appropriate role of the courts versus the role of the jury.

In the days before jury trials, it was well-settled law that the determination of "obviousness" (whether the invention was obvious in light of the prior art) was a matter of law for the court, whereas anticipation (whether a prior art reference read exactly on the claims of the patent) was a matter for the trier of fact. Since the trier of fact and the court were one and the same in those cases, the only technical legal impact of that distinction was that theoretically obviousness would be a question for de novo review by the court of appeals, whereas anticipation would be subject to the clearly erroneous test.

In reality, this was a distinction without a difference, because the courts of appeals (each court of appeals had jurisdiction over the district court's decisions within its circuit) would treat the determination of obviousness as though it were really subject to the clearly erroneous test. That is, the courts gave great deference to the trier of fact and the trier of fact's ability to understand and appreciate the demeanor of the witnesses, where those witnesses were expert witnesses. Some courts of appeals, of course, treated their role as the right to grant de novo review seriously and actually imposed their judgment over that of the trial court on the question of obviousness.

To my knowledge, no intelligent reason has ever been set forth as to why obviousness should be a matter of law for the court and anticipation should be a matter of fact for the trier of fact. Nonetheless, this was the state of the law, and it was not really much of a problem because, as a practical matter, a court was deciding both issues. With the creation of the CAFC, whose jurisdiction extends to all patent appeals, this changed dramatically. Instead of having each separate court of appeals able to make its own determination on obviousness, all of these determinations went to one court, which, as it happened, became very much pro-patent. In the past, many of the circuit courts of appeals had a very negative view of patents, viewing them as fundamentally anticompetitive and suspect in light of the antitrust laws. Accordingly, they threw them out right and left as well as up and down. The CAFC, which included a number of patent lawyers, suddenly began upholding patents. Patent infringement litigation became far more attractive, particularly to the plaintiff's bar.

As a result, everyone and his brother began filing patent infringement cases and demanding jury trials. Once again, as a practical matter, not many of these cases actually got to trial, because the vast majority of patent infringement cases (like all cases) settled. Nonetheless, there was a clear trend in a new direction. This created unsettling problems, because we now had obviousness to be decided by the court and anticipation to be decided by the jury. Once again, as a practical matter, many courts simply present the question of obviousness to the jury in the form of an interrogatory and then adopt the jury's findings. Nonetheless, under the present state of the law, a trial judge has the right to overrule a jury's conclusion and substitute his or her own judgment on the issue of obviousness. With regard to anticipation, however, the jury's determination is final (unless it is clearly not supportable by any of the evidence), and the judge cannot simply substitute his or her judgment.

Claim Interpretation

Another area where there has been some confusion between the role of the court and the role of the jury or trier of fact is claim interpretation. Claim interpretation is a matter of law for the court. The court determines the meaning of terms in the claims by reference to the plain meaning of the words, the specification, the file history, and, if the court decides it is necessary, expert testimony. This rule of law was reaffirmed by the CAFC and the Supreme Court in the case of *Markman v. Westview Instruments, Inc.*, 517 U.S. 370 (1996).

As a result of the *Markman* case, there were great cries of anguish and exclamations of rejoicing and despair from various corners, all claiming that the *Markman* decision would virtually eliminate the role of the jury. In other words, many patent lawyers were of the belief (a mistaken one, in my view) that the resolution of the interpretation in the meaning of claims by the court would automatically determine the issue of infringement. The court would merely take the accused item and match it to the claims as interpreted by the court and determine whether there was infringement. This has resulted in a rash of so-called Markman hearings, where the courts have decided claim interpretation. These often have been quickly followed by or incorporated with motions for summary judgment.

I'll admit to having been somewhat skeptical of the wisdom of the *Markman* decision, because I personally am a great believer in trial by jury. I recently had an experience, however, that caused me to rethink my position. I had been litigating a case for more than four years at a cost of many millions of dollars to my client. It was a case that revolved directly around claim interpretation. The court had refused to rule on the meaning of the terms in the claims during the entire pendency of the action. At the time *Markman* was decided by the CAFC, the court indicated that it would be willing to take a good, hard look at the meaning of the terms in the claims. Right about that time, the Supreme Court granted certiorari in *Markman*, and the court postponed taking any action until the Supreme Court's decision. Once the Supreme Court affirmed *Markman*, the court immediately scheduled a Markman hearing on claim interpretation. Both sides filed their briefs in support of their positions on the meaning of the claims. It was obvious that the plaintiff (the other side) could not possibly win its case on infringement unless it was able to persuade the court to agree with its interpretation of the claims.

As I indicated above, one factor the court is supposed to take into consideration in determining the meaning of terms in a claim is the file history. In this particular case, there was some ambiguity in the actual language of the claims, and if they were read in a vacuum, the plaintiff's position might very well make sense. When read in light of the statements made by the patent attorney to the Patent Office, however, it was obvious that the plaintiff's interpretation of the claims could not possibly prevail. In fact, statements were made by the patent attorney that were precisely on point and that established conclusively that the interpretation being sought by the plaintiff was not that presented to the Patent Office.

The plaintiff in that case did everything within its power to prevent the claim interpretation from being decided by the court. After I saw its papers, I knew why. It was hoping to fool a jury, by providing enough irrelevant and confusing scientific data, into accepting its interpretation of the claims. It was quite obvious that anyone sophisticated in file histories (as was the judge in this particular case) would not buy the plaintiff's version for a nanosecond. The plaintiff's position was absolutely without merit, but without the safeguard of a judge's interpreting the claims, there was the distinct possibility that a jury might have fallen victim to the plaintiff's devious plot. I was never so glad to have a Markman hearing in my life.

Almost on the heels of the *Markman* decision, however, the CAFC came down with the *Hilton-Davis* case, which established, in no uncertain terms, that infringement was a matter for the trier of fact. It also determined that the doctrine of equivalents (which will be discussed later) was a matter for determination by the jury.

All of a sudden the patent bar found itself back to square one. Can a court really interpret claims and a jury really determine infringement? Further confusion ensued when the Supreme Court granted certiorari in *Hilton-Davis*. This resulted in widespread suicides among patent lawyers, who can't stand uncertainty of any sort. For 800 years the Supreme Court had left patent lawyers alone, and now it wants to run their lives. This is viewed by most patent lawyers as a violation of their constitutional right to privacy.

An example of the kind of confusion that can result from this question of judicial claim interpretation in light of *Markman* occurred in a case that I tried to a jury just before the *Markman* decision was entered. In that case, the judge decided the meaning of a number of terms in the claims, but he did not decide all of them. He then sent the case to the jury with an instruction regarding certain terms in the claims. The defendant contended that those terms meant one thing and we contended that they meant another. There was expert testimony on both sides reaching diametrically opposite conclusions as to what the particular terms meant.

The judge did not send this to the jury with an interrogatory for them to come back with their interpretation of the claim language, but merely gave them an instruction to make a determination as to whether there was infringement. Accordingly, there was nothing on the record to indicate what those claims were interpreted to mean by the jury, and there was no interpretation of them by the court. In the court's ruling on the post-trial motions, the court decided the meaning of the claim terms and said the jury's verdict was consistent with his ruling, so he allowed the verdict to stand.

In light of all of this information, when your client comes to you and says, "Will this patent case be tried to a jury?," you can truthfully answer, "Well, you have asked a very interesting question." Then you can proceed to give him the totally confusing explanation that I have just given to you.

Now, obviously, all of these confusing issues would not exist in the event you were to try your case to a judge and not a jury. Of course, either side can demand trial by jury. It may happen, however, that your opponent will want to try the case to a judge and may approach you to see if you would stipulate doing so.

This brings us to our next topic.

8

Do I Really Want to Try This Case to a Judge?

I recently attended a seminar where the guest speakers consisted of a panel of federal judges and one state court judge. At one point in the seminar, a senior federal judge asked how those of us who practice patent law determine whether we are going to try a case to a jury or to a judge. No one was raising his or her hand, so to fill the embarrassing silence, I foolishly raised mine and volunteered that under no circumstances, given a choice, would I try a case to a judge.

Another judge on the panel looked at me with incredulity and queried, "Why?"

My foolishly brave response was, "I don't trust them." I am sure from the expressions on the faces of the members of the panel that they felt I was attacking their integrity. I quickly pointed out that I was not attacking their integrity but merely the process. I was then asked by another member of the panel if I didn't feel that juries often went off on tangents and decided cases based on their feelings about someone's hairstyle. My response was that after having interviewed hundreds of jurors over the course of 27 years (at that time) in the practice of law, I had never found one who decided a case based on anything other than his or her analysis of the facts. This, of course, does not mean that their analysis was always correct, but the attitude of many members of the judiciary was reflected by that judge's question. In other words, there is a certain amount of judicial arrogance: Judges think that they pay attention to the facts but jurors often go off on tangents that have nothing to do with the case. This belief of mine was further demonstrated by one of the judges, who expressed his opinion that lawyers try cases to jurors when they want to rely on confusion, and they try them to judges when they want to rely on the facts. That particular judge's statement was a perfect example of why I don't trust judges.

Incidentally, Gerry Spence, in his book (which I highly recommend), *How to Argue and Win Every Time,* gives judges a rather rough time. While I do not agree with all of his analysis and impressions of the judiciary, I do believe that in many respects he is right on the mark.

Judges vs. Juries

This is a particular concern in intellectual property cases. What I have often found in my practice is that judges will quickly assume that they understand the facts, and it is thereafter very difficult to get them to look at the case in any light other than their initial impression. I have also found that judges are often very slow when it comes to understanding technology.

On the other hand, I have found that jurors are not quick to form impressions; that they pay careful attention to the lawyers; that they do not assume that they know anything; and that they often are far better able to understand complex technology than are judges, whose background is primarily in the area of liberal arts. This is not to be misconstrued as a belief that all jurors make correct decisions or pay attention to the evidence, the O. J. Simpson case being a dramatic case in point. I do believe, however, that criminal cases are in a class by themselves and that jurors bring much personal baggage to these cases. In intellectual property cases, the juries generally have no feeling one way or the other about the parties, and they are truly capable of being objective.

Another question that was posed to me by one of the judges on the panel was whether it was not very difficult to explain complex technology to the great ignorant mass of laypeople who sit on juries (not his exact words). I explained to the judge that if an opening statement is done properly, this should not be a problem.

In fact, this is true. My technique for determining that I am fully and adequately explaining the technology to the jury is to use mock juries, and often I will simply take individuals from all walks of life, including friends, coworkers, secretaries, receptionists, and strangers on the street. I explain the technology to them in as much detail as I can and in a manner that I hope is understandable to these individuals and groups, and then I have them explain it back to me. Once I have reached the point where I can give an opening statement to any person and that person can basically give that opening statement back to me, then I know I am ready for a jury. I also make extensive use of exhibits in opening statements, including building devices, taking devices apart, handing them to the jury, and letting the jury pass them around. While some judges may be appalled at this, I have found that most judges are receptive to it, and most savvy patent lawyers will stipulate to it because they want to do the same thing.

Another consideration in determining whether to try a case to a judge or jury in patent cases is the fact that there are a great many judicial safeguards. For example, in *Markman*, the jury rendered a verdict of infringement, and the court subsequently reached a different conclusion from the jury about claim interpretation and then said, based on the court's claim interpretation, there could be no infringement; it then reversed the jury's decision. This action by the court was upheld by the CAFC.

Another reason for taking a case to a jury instead of a judge is that, frankly, it is much easier to try a case to a judge than to a jury. An experienced jury trial lawyer who knows the rules of evidence and who knows how to object and when to object is not going to be caught napping while inappropriate questions are asked and answered. This is a tremendous advantage over a lawyer who has limited jury trial experience and who is used to relying on the judge's discretion to "filter the evidence." I have always thought this was a rather disingenuous concept, wherein the trier of fact hears the evidence and then determines what evidence he will consider or not consider. Judges are human, too, and there is often a problem with judges hearing things they should not hear and being influenced by them. An experienced and competent jury trial lawyer will never let a jury hear things that the jury should not hear and that may affect its judgment.

Two-Tier Litigation Team

Because many patent lawyers do not have extensive jury trial experience, a number of corporations have attempted to use a two-tier litigation team. They use an experienced jury trial lawyer to present the case and a patent lawyer to provide the backup and the workup of the case.

There are some instances where this teamwork approach works very well. There are other times, however, when it works very poorly. It is obviously preferable to have one lawyer who is both an experienced jury trial lawyer and a knowledgeable patent lawyer. The problem with having a non-patent lawyer handle a case in front of a jury is that there may be times when an objection is called for, the determination must be made instantly, and the non-patent lawyer does not have enough familiarity with the subject matter and intuitive sense of whether a question is appropriate, and will miss making an objection in a timely fashion. I have seen this occur time and time again. It is a question of not knowing what you don't know, and, of course, the patent lawyer who is sitting at counsel table cannot leap up and make an objection, because courts will allow only one lawyer at a time to handle the witness.

Another problem arises in cases of this nature when patent lawyers write out opening statements and experienced non-patent trial lawyers begin to read those statements to a jury only to find themselves interrupted and their opening statements objected to because they are argumentative. I have made such objections in cases and have been very successful in throwing the non-patent lawyer off stride. The problem is that treading that thin line between opening statement and argument requires a great deal of experience. When the patent lawyer who is writing the opening statement is not an experienced jury trial lawyer, the tendency and the temptation is to go way over the line and write arguments into the opening statement. The non-patent jury trial lawyer who then reads that statement is not fully aware of the significance of what he or she is saying.

I was trying a case once against a team of patent and non-patent lawyers where the experienced and highly competent jury trial lawyer was basically reading an opening statement prepared for him by inexperienced (at jury trial work) patent lawyers. I was able to object successfully to his opening statement on three or four different occasions, which caused him to lose his place in the script, resulting in long and embarrassing pauses and a completely ineffective opening statement.

In any event, these are calls that have to be made on a case-by-case basis, but the general practice lawyer or the in-house corporate counsel who has to make these kinds of decisions should be aware of the ramifications and the pitfalls of approaching these cases in terms of deciding whether to try them to a jury and, if they are going to be tried to a jury, how the case should be managed, handled, and presented.

I would say that jury trial cases are substantially more difficult to try; they require much greater technical expertise, and most of all, they require the ability to think and act instantaneously. Jury trials are a constant dynamic process, and no matter how much we try to keep them under control by pretrial preparation, pretrial orders, etc., they are still going to be filled with surprises at every turn. The lawyer who is good at this has a substantial advantage over the lawyer who may have great mastery of the subject matter in the law but who is inflexible and unable to think and act quickly. On the other hand, a lawyer who is able to think quickly but does not have knowledge of the technology and the law is at a major disadvantage as well.

The obvious answer is that if you are going to try jury trial cases, you should be able to think quickly on your feet and you should have encyclopedic knowledge of the law in this area, as well as a thorough understanding of the rules of evidence and the ability to make adjustments on a second-by-second basis as the case ebbs and flows and moves in your direction one minute and in the bad guy's direction the next.

Assuming you have a choice about whether to try the case to a jury or to a judge, the conventional wisdom is that if you represent a large corporate defendant against a plaintiff who is seeking substantial damages, you should attempt to have the case tried to a judge, because judges tend to be much more conservative and less influenced by the respective size of the parties. While this is certainly a justifiable position, the first problem with it is that a knowledgeable plaintiff will always want a jury for exactly that reason. My personal view (which I admit is not shared by many in my profession) is that even when I represent a large corporation, I prefer to try the case to a jury.

Judicial Safeguards

In an antitrust case that I tried (*Jacobson v. Kawasaki*, No. 89-2008 (C. Dist. Cal. 1991), the case was tried to a jury, which brought back a substantial judgment in favor of the plaintiff. This was distressing to me, because I represented Kawasaki. Fortunately, the jury had come back in Kawasaki's favor on every cause of action for which Jacobson had a theoretically valid cause of action. For example, the jury threw out a number of causes of actions based on the statutes of limitations. They did this in the face of the conventional wisdom that juries will disregard statutes of limitations if they feel that they want to reach a certain result.

As it turned out, the one cause of action on which the jury awarded a substantial sum was one for which there was no supporting evidence. Now, while this may seem an example of a jury running amuck, to me this was another example of why it is safe to rely on judicial safeguards. The judge in that case was John G. Davies (the same judge who presided over the second Rodney King beating trial), and he wisely threw out the jury's verdict and ordered a new trial. Midway through the new trial, the parties reached a settlement.

While this was a somewhat scary experience, I was nonetheless heartened by the fact that the jury did pay attention to the law regarding the statute of limitations and basically did the right thing, and in the one area where the jury made a fundamental mistake, there was a judicial safeguard in place to prevent that runaway car from flying over the cliff. (Please excuse the dramatic analogy.) One last thought on the matter of jury versus judge: While jurors are generally just as good as, if not better than, judges in analyzing and determining the facts in a case, one area in which I believe there is an advantage to a judge is that judges, as a result of having seen many, many people testify, may be less affected by matters such as personality, body language, and so on.

Impact of Witnessess

With this thought in mind, it may behoove a lawyer who is straddling the fence on whether to go jury or nonjury to take into consideration the impact that his chief witnesses are likely to have on a jury. For example, I tried a case involving alleged infringement of a patent in which I represented the defendant. That case was tried to a jury, and the inventor, who was a university professor, made a very bad impression on the jury. He was particularly arrogant and appeared to talk down to the jury, and was also very quick to argue with me during cross-examination. I felt fairly confident that we had won the case when, after the inventor had responded to a particular question, I noticed a number of the jurors shake their heads and roll their eyes, and a couple of the other jurors stared at him with open-mouthed disbelief. His arrogance had caused him to refuse to concede even the most minute point, and it soon became obvious that the jury gave him no credence whatsoever—even in those areas where he theoretically might have deserved some. I believe that had he been my witness, I either would not have tried the case to a jury or I would have worked on him extensively and found those areas where it would be important to concede, rather than attempt to defend on every point and thereby lose total credibility. I suspect that a court might not have been as inclined to tune out this witness as the jury was. I still believe that a court would have reached the same conclusion, as the facts were solidly on our side, as was later determined by the Court of Appeals for the Federal Circuit (*Beachcombers v. Wildwood Creative Products,* 31 F.3d 1154 (Fed Cir. 1994)).

You now know more than you will ever need or want to know about juries and judges in patent infringement litigation. Congratulations!

9

Expert Witnesses

I suppose you are saying, "Why do I need to read about expert witnesses in patent law? This is supposed to be a primer for those of us who do not know anything about patent law, and I'm certainly never going to try a patent case." In the first place, you may be wrong; you may try a patent case someday. But beyond that, this is something I want to write about and if you don't want to read it, that's fine.

Alternatively, you may be asking yourself, "Why do I need to know anything about expert witnesses in patent infringement cases? I've tried plenty of cases, and I know everything there is to know about expert witnesses anyway." While I probably cannot disagree with you in that regard, I do believe there are some peculiarities about expert witnesses in patent cases, and technology cases in general, of which you might want to be aware.

In-house Experts

The first principle of which you need to be aware is that in most patent cases the best experts are found in-house. That is, if you are on the side of the patent holder, then the inventor himself or herself may very well be your best expert witness, not only in explaining the technology but also in terms of testifying as to infringement. Remember, on infringement you don't need to have an expert saying, "In my opinion there is infringement." In fact, many courts will not allow that kind of testimony. What the courts will allow is for an expert to say, "I understand the product that is accused of infringing, and it contains element A, which matches element A of claim 1," etc.

It is also nice, psychologically, to be able to have the inventor himself carry the burden of the case. It gets away from the notion that you have gone out and obtained the services of a hired gun. Also, if the technology is state-of-the-art, then it may very well be that your client's in-house technical people may be the best in the country to discuss the particular subject matter. In fact, they may be among the few in the world who really understand the technology well enough to discuss it in court.

If you are representing the accused infringing party, then the same also may hold true—particularly if your client's in-house technical personnel evaluated the technology before your client decided to build the accused product and concluded that it is different in some material respect from that in the patent.

Before going further in discussing the in-house technical experts, I should point out that there are really two classes of liability experts in patent cases.[1] The first class consists of technical experts and the second class consists of legal experts. Patent law is one of the few areas of the law where lawyers are actually allowed to testify as experts, although this trend is diminishing considerably as more of these cases are tried to a jury. In the past, when these cases were tried to judges, judges often would use the services of patent lawyers as witnesses to help the judge understand the issues. In jury trial cases, however, there is a whole different dynamic, and there is always a legitimate concern that the jury may be inappropriately persuaded by a lawyer's testimony.

My personal preference is not to use lawyers as experts except to explain the operations of the Patent Office and to explain the basics of a patent, how it is obtained, the significance of claims versus preferred embodiment, etc. I personally never put a patent lawyer on the stand to give his or her opinion that claims in a patent are valid or invalid or are infringed or not infringed.

I had one case where the lawyers for the defendant had built their entire noninfringement case around the testimony and opinion of a well-established and nationally recognized patent lawyer. It was their intention to put him on the stand and basically give the closing argument. I objected to their use of this lawyer in this regard, and when my objection

---

1. There are also damage experts, but here we are only discussing liability.

was sustained, the other side's lawyer blurted out in anguish that their entire case of noninfringement was built around their expert lawyer's testimony. This is an example of poor planning. Even if they intended to use this lawyer in this way, they should have had a ready backup plan available.

They, of course, were still able to argue noninfringement, but their argument was to no avail. I personally do not think that the lawyer's testimony would have won the day for them, but had they been allowed to use him, they would certainly have endured a little less psychological pain. As it turned out, that lawyer not only was unable to give the noninfringement opinion they wanted, but in cross-examination I actually got him to concede that basically all of the elements for infringement under the doctrine of equivalents (to be discussed later) were present.

Even if you have outstanding in-house technical people to act as expert witnesses, in my opinion it is always advisable to retain an outside expert. In the first place, you may have more of an opportunity to interview outside experts and select the one who suits you best. Universities are always excellent places to look for outstanding experts, and occasionally one even finds a university professor who can teach. For example, in the O. J. Simpson trial, Dr. Cotton, who testified as a DNA expert on behalf of the prosecution, was a perfect example of an outstanding expert. She was straightforward, she was understandable to most jurors (the sitting jury in that case being the glaring exception), and she was very pleasant and personable and, most important of all, not the least bit condescending. She also knew her stuff.

Lawyers as Experts

Now, you are probably asking yourselves, "With all these experts, who is the most important expert in the case?" Okay, maybe you weren't asking yourself that question; but if you had been, I would have answered, "The lawyer."

As I indicated previously, opening statements should basically present the entire case, including a detailed explanation of all the technology that is going to be presented to the jury. You should not only explain the technology from your client's perspective but also tell the jury what the other side is going to contend. To do this, the lawyer who is delivering the opening statement must have a complete and total understanding of the technology and also must be able to explain it to the jury in a manner that it can understand.

Under no circumstances should a lawyer ever read an opening statement. This is particularly true when you are dealing with technology, where you are picking up the devices, taking them apart, reassembling them, and handing them to the jury. In one case, I actually performed an experiment in front of the jury during the opening statement. I videotaped the experiment in front of the jury as it was watching and then, when I was presenting my case, I introduced that tape into evidence. The jury members then were able to take that tape, which they had actually seen prepared during opening statement, back into the jury room with them during deliberations. In other words, I actually prepared evidence during an opening statement.

The Challenge of Confidentiality

There is another reason why the lawyer is the most important expert in the case. That reason is the confidentiality order that is often found in these cases. In fact, it is almost universally found in these cases, and I can't think of a single technology case I've tried in 30-some years in which such an order was not used. The problem with protective orders is that they sometimes prevent lawyers from discussing some of the most important information in a case with their clients. This is particularly a problem when the client is providing most of the experts. It is even more of a problem when technology is state-of-the-art and few people besides the client actually have enough technical familiarity with the subject matter to be able to provide appropriate testimony.

While the lawyers can always use in-house personnel to deal with the affirmative case that they intend to present and to deal with evidence that originates with the client (for example, the patent and all of the technological material that led to the obtaining of the patent), the lawyer still will find herself adrift and on her own when it comes to analyzing the technical information that has been obtained from the other side in discovery.

On more than one occasion, I have found myself at a distinct advantage in a case when I had become thoroughly familiar with the technology before discovery and the lawyer on the other side had no understanding of the technology and was barred by the protective order from obtaining guidance and information from his client. In one particular case, a lawyer sought relief from the protective order on precisely those grounds. It was a case where the lawyer did not have a technical background (it was a trade secret case) and entered into a stipulation for protective order without giving any thought to the fact that he had no independent ability to read and understand the information that he would be obtaining from my client in the normal course of discovery. We settled that case in short order.

What does this mean to the general practitioner who may find himself involved in representing and guiding a client in a patent infringement or other technology-related case? What it means is you must make sure you pick your patent lawyer very carefully. If the case is one involving solid-state circuits, you'd better make darn sure that the lawyers handling the case have a solid background in electronics and can understand and deal with the technology independently of what assistance and guidance they may receive from an expert. This is particularly important advice to keep in mind, because lawyers are notorious for passing things off to experts and allowing experts to run their cases, particularly if the cases involve areas in which the lawyers themselves have little or no expertise. A lawyer in technology cases in general and in patent infringement cases, in particular, cannot afford the luxury of relying on someone else's technological expertise.

Of course, there is one very vital reason why a lawyer needs to be an expert on the technology, and that is because he or she must cross-examine the other side's experts. There is nothing scarier than a lawyer who goes into a trial of a case not knowing what she does not know.

Taking Depositions

When taking the other side's expert's deposition, you should always endeavor to bring your own expert with you. In that case, should you miss asking important questions or need to follow up on certain lines of inquiry, you at least would have your own expert there to give you advice and counseling. After having taken the other side's expert's deposition, you and your expert should then carefully go over the questions that you would want to be asking that expert on cross-examination in front of the jury. I personally like to use my expert as a foil and practice cross-examining him as part of my trial preparation.

Role of the Nontechnical Lawyer

Where does this leave the general practitioner or in-house corporate counsel who has no technical background and who is steering his client through the uncharted waters of patent infringement litigation? If you are not a technical person and do not understand the technology or the technical details of the patent, this does not mean that there is not an appropriate role for you throughout all stages of the trial, including discovery and the trial itself. You should, at a minimum, obtain an ongoing series of briefings from your lawyer and your experts. I have found that no matter how difficult the technology, the basic concepts are understandable once a person puts aside her math and science phobias. (These phobias are particularly prevalent among people who went to law school to avoid having to study math or science. You know who I'm talking about. I'm talking about you!)

I have often found the input and advice from outside counsel with no technical background to be extremely valuable. This is particularly true because these cases are not tried to technical people (unless, of course, they are being tried in Silicon Valley), and therefore even simple words and phrases that are routinely used by people familiar with certain areas of technology may be completely foreign to other persons. General counsel are often very helpful in pointing out these areas.

I once had a case where the in-house lawyer on the other side was complaining to me that his patent counsel was constantly speaking in tongues. As an example, he said that his patent counsel constantly referred to "scems." He told me that when he finally asked what the term "scems" referred to, he was informed that his counsel meant schematics. He then confided in me that he was embarrassed to ask what "schematic" meant. I was at first a little surprised because I thought everyone knew what a schematic was, and then, in an unusual display of gentlemanliness (for me), I explained it to him so that he would be able to follow the discussions and the testimony. I thought this was a rather interesting example of the importance of communication between nontechnical counsel and patent counsel. Since most of these cases are brought to patent counsel by general counsel or by a company's outside general practice lawyer, it is extremely important that all of these lawyers learn to speak the same language. The bottom line is that the lawyer must be more of an expert than any other person in the case, and there are no shortcuts.

10

Patent Prosecutors as Witnesses

For years it has been a common practice to take the depositions of lawyers who wrote and prosecuted patent applications that matured into a patent that became the subject matter of the lawsuit. It is now pretty well established that the attorney-client privilege extends to virtually all communications between the applicant and the lawyer. Accordingly, the only matters about which the patent lawyer can be questioned are matters relating to the public record, that is, the prosecution history. In that regard, the prosecution history speaks for itself. The patent lawyer cannot broaden the claims or change the claims or change the meaning of the claims based upon his impressions, views, or intent.

The only exception to the relevance of the testimony of the patent prosecutor would be in a situation where there was a suspicion of a crime or a commission of a fraud. In such an instance, the attorney-client privilege evaporates, and the patent prosecutor could theoretically be deposed and forced to testify concerning communications with his or her client. Obviously, these situations are extremely rare.

For the above reasons, I am very protective of patent prosecutors when it comes to the taking of their depositions. If I am defending the deposition of a prosecutor, I will not allow that prosecutor to answer any questions relating to any communications with his or her client (which is usually my client also by that time). This limits the deposition basically to matters that are already in the public record. Accordingly, most of those depositions are a waste of time; I personally almost never take the deposition of the prosecutor, and I almost never call a prosecutor as a witness.

11

Infringement

Direct

As alluded to earlier, a patent is not simply a technical document that one obtains because it has a neat ribbon on the front and can be used to decorate the wall. The only real function of a patent is its use as a trial exhibit. Accordingly, the active involvement of a patent has to do with the infringement of a product. Because a patent gives the patent owner the exclusive right to make, use, and sell the patented product, the making, use, and/or sale by another person constitutes infringement. Again, contrary to popular wisdom, what is infringed is not the "patent," but specific claims of a patent. Because the claims of a patent are meant to cover a number of variations on the preferred embodiment, all of which hopefully embody the principles of the invention, different claims may be applicable to different products.

In doing the fundamental claims analysis of an accused or suspected product, one normally prepares a claims chart. (Failure to prepare a claims chart before filing suit may subject one to the risk of being accused of sham litigation or abuse of process.) A claims chart is prepared simply by taking each of the elements of the claim and applying them to the accused or suspected product. If a claim contains a number of elements, such as "a widget comprising elements A, B, and C," then one takes the accused product to see if, first, it is a widget and, second, it has elements

A, B, and C. If it contains each of those elements, then it is a directly infringing product.

One common misconception is that one may avoid infringement by adding elements. In other words, the accused product contains elements A, B, and C, and also D. The mere addition of element D does not defeat infringement. The only way you can defeat infringement is by having less, not more. In other words, if one has a product containing elements A, B, and C that may infringe a patent claim, then the elimination of element A and the substitution of element X for element A may very well create a noninfringing product.

It is in this fundamental claims analysis that the broadening and narrowing of claims become important considerations. The broader the claim, the greater the likelihood that products will read upon, or infringe, that claim. The narrower the claim, the less likelihood there is of a product infringing. This is because, for example, if the broad claim contained the language "A; B affixed to A, . . ." and the narrower claim was "A; B affixed to A by a screw . . . ," then a product that fastened by means of a nail would infringe the broader claim, but would not infringe the narrower claim.

The question then, of course, is why ever bother with a narrow claim when that simply will make it more difficult to prove infringement? The answer is that broader claims are more easily attacked as invalid based on prior art, whereas narrower claims, while more easily defended on the basis of infringement, are also usually more difficult to attack based on prior art. This issue, then, is over claim interpretation as it relates to validity and infringement, and the issue of which claims are to be asserted presents a constant source of tension and a dynamic within patent infringement litigation.

Where any particular claim is concerned, the plaintiff will argue for one interpretation, depending on the prior art that is out there and the particular structure of the accused infringing device, and the defendant will argue for another. If the prior art is very close to the claim, then the plaintiff will probably be arguing for a narrow interpretation of the claim, and the defendant will be arguing for a broad interpretation of the claim to defeat the patent. On the other hand, when the plaintiff argues for a narrow interpretation of the claim, the plaintiff then may find it that much more difficult to prove its infringement case. By the same token, the defendant, by arguing for a broad interpretation of the claim (to make it easier to have the claim thrown out altogether), runs the risk that it will be easier to show infringement.

At some point in time, a party needs to fish or cut bait and determine which way it is going to attempt to have the claims interpreted.

More often than not (in my experience), the parties unashamedly and unabashedly put forward contradictory positions until the last possible minute in litigation. I have even seen parties assert completely contradictory positions (or at least attempt to do so) throughout the trial. I have seen defendants attempt to assert that the claims should be interpreted broadly where prior art is concerned but narrowly where infringement is concerned. Of course, they cannot have it both ways, but it is amazing how many people try. (Sometimes just being intellectually honest with oneself can result in an amazing reduction—or increase—in stress.)

Claims generally are divided into two classes, independent claims and dependent claims. An independent claim speaks for itself. It is a self-contained unit when each and every one of the elements is set forth. A dependent claim is one that incorporates, by reference, all of the elements of a previous claim but then narrows that claim by, for example, stating "wherein A is affixed to B by screws." Most of the argument usually revolves around how to interpret the language of particular claims. Once that language has been determined (as by, for example, a Markman hearing), then it is simply a question of looking at the accused device to see if it contains each and every element of the claims.

We will leave this topic for now, but we will return to it when we discuss the "doctrine of equivalents."

Contributory and Inducement of Infringement

Now you know there is such a thing as "direct infringement." This is the infringement of which most people think when they think of patent infringement. There are, however, two other kinds of infringement that are probably, for many purposes, more important than direct infringement. They are (as has already been hinted in the title) contributory infringement and inducement of infringement.

The first thing you should know about each of these kinds of infringement is that they both require intent. In other words, to be guilty of either of these infringements, a person must know of the existence of the patent and must knowingly engage in conduct that either contributes to infringement by someone else or induces another person to infringe. These are, in essence, willful and deliberate torts, which become very important when seeking to have the case declared an exceptional case so as to entitle one to attorney's fees and possibly treble damages. These torts also have significance in other, related areas such as antitrust, willful and tortious interference with a prospective business advantage, and so on.

Contributory Infringement

Contributory infringement involves the manufacture and sale of a product that is intended to be incorporated into an infringing product. A defense to contributory infringement is that the accused article is a staple article of commerce. In other words, if someone is selling penny nails and one of the customers is using those nails to construct an infringing product, the seller of the nails is not liable as a contributory infringer. On the other hand, if the accused infringer is making a specialized product intended specifically to be used in the infringing product, that constitutes contributory infringement.

An example of contributory infringement involved a case I had concerning water bottles for use with water coolers. The patent was on an apparatus that included caps with specially designed plugs to operate in conjunction with water coolers equipped with probes specially designed to fit with the plugs in the caps to allow dispensation of liquid when in the open position and resealing of the caps when the container was empty.

The accused infringer was making caps with plugs in them that were only part of the system. These caps with plugs were sold to sellers of bottled water, who put them on the bottles and shipped them to their customers, who put them on water coolers containing the probes. In other words, the only direct infringers were the people who were actually using the entire assembly. Because the caps with plugs were specifically designed for use in the infringing combination, I was able to successfully maintain a cause of action for contributory patent infringement against the manufacturer of the caps. In that particular case, there was no question about knowledge on the part of the infringer because they were well aware of the patent, and there had been substantial correspondence back and forth before the filing of the lawsuit.

"Inducement of infringement" consists of the act of encouraging others to infringe. This usually involves advertising or may even involve sets of instructions that are sent along with an infringing product. To understand this concept, it should be borne in mind that there may be more than one infringer along the line. For example, the manufacturer of the infringing product is one infringer, and the customer of the manufacturer who thereafter uses the product can be a second infringer. Accordingly, a manufacturer who sells a product and then advertises and/or sends instructions to consumers to encourage those people to use the infringing product in an infringing manner may very well be liable for inducing infringement.

In other words, a person may be both a direct infringer and an inducer of infringement. The same is not true, however, with contributory infringement. By definition, a contributory infringer is not a direct infringer as to the particular product being accused of infringement.

Can a person be a contributory infringer and an inducer as well? The answer to this, of course, is yes. If a person is selling a contributory infringing part and is advertising and/or sending instructions or otherwise engaged in encouraging people to utilize its infringing parts in conjunction with an overall infringing product, this constitutes both contributory infringement and inducement of infringement.

All of these causes of action may spin off into general unfair competition, tortious interference with a prospective business advantage, and so on.

Who Owns the Rights to a Patent?

The inventor owns the rights to a patent unless the inventor is employed and the invention occurs during the course and scope of the inventor's employment activities.

If the employed inventor invents something on his or her own time, even though that employee may be using expertise obtained while on the job, that invention and the patent rights belong to the employee. Often employers will insure against that possibility by having a provision in employment contracts that prohibits an employee from having any patent rights while so employed. There is sometimes a question as to the legal viability of those types of contracts, but they are not uncommon.

12

Doctrine of Equivalents

The doctrine of equivalents was specifically designed to drive lawyers nuts, and it has succeeded.

The doctrine of equivalents is a doctrine that is intended (as are, theoretically, all equity doctrines) to prevent a miscarriage of justice. The miscarriage of justice, in this particular circumstance, consists of the attempt by a potential infringer to avoid infringement by making a meaningless or incidental change in the device that still affords the infringer all of the benefits of the teaching of the patent.

If you are in possession of my first book, please turn to the chapter on the doctrine of equivalents and then, with a razor blade, remove it in its entirety. As they say in my office, "That chapter is sooo fifteen minutes ago." It's obsolete, it's wrong, it's useless, and it's misleading. There are probably a lot of other appropriate adjectives as well, but I've been sick, so I'm going easy on myself.

The doctrine of equivalents was invented and developed by the courts so that the various judges on the Court of Appeals for the Federal Circuit (CAFC) would have something about which to argue among themselves and also to provide a basis for contention between the CAFC and the Supreme Court. It has achieved those goals with remarkable success. For example, during the oral argument before the Supreme Court in the case of *Festo Corp. v. Shoketsu Kinzoku Kogyo Kabushiki Co.*, 122 S. Ct

1831 (2002), the Chief Justice was heard to remark,[1] "I dare say we're in a better position to interpret our cases than the Federal Circuit."

So, now, what exactly is the doctrine of equivalents?

The doctrine of equivalents is a doctrine by which one can be found guilty of infringement of a claim in a patent, even if that person is not guilty of literal infringement. In order for there to be literal infringement, every element of a claim must be found in the accused infringing device. If any single element is missing, then there is no infringement. The addition of elements to an accused infringing product is not a defense to infringement. In other words, if one has a patent claim that covers the elements of an automobile but does not include a hood ornament, making a device that contains all of the elements of the claims and then has an additional hood ornament does not avoid infringement. If, however, one is able to remove one of the elements (such as the engine) of the claim of which the person is accused of infringement, then that person will avoid infringement. An important thing to remember is that an infringement analysis is a claim element by claim element analysis. In other words, one does not look to the claims as a whole or to an accused infringing device as a whole.

Purpose of the Doctrine

The doctrine of equivalents was designed to prevent a potential infringer from making an insignificant change to one or more of the features of a device in order to achieve all of the advantages of all of the elements of the claims in the invention and yet not be guilty of literal infringement. If the changes or modifications are insignificant, it would be a manifest injustice to allow a person to avoid infringement in this manner. Accordingly, the doctrine of equivalents was created to avoid that injustice. Under the doctrine of equivalents, analysis is still done on a claim element by claim element basis. The difference is that if a particular claim element is not found literally in an accused infringing device, but there is an element in the accused infringing device that performs essentially the same function in essentially the same manner to accomplish essentially the same result as the particular claim ele-

---

1. Even as we speak, the CAFC has decided to have an en banc hearing to determine whether the issues for which the case was remanded by the Supreme Court are issues of fact to be determined by the trial judge or issues of law to be decided by the CAFC. By the time you read this chapter, that decision will already have been made.

ment, then that part of the accused infringing device will be held to have read upon that particular claim element. If each claim element is found in an accused infringing device either directly or under the doctrine of equivalents, it infringes.

A while back there was some controversy over the question of who should decide doctrine of equivalents issues, a judge or a jury. The law is now well settled that infringement, including infringement under the doctrine of equivalents, is a determination for the trier of fact, that is, a jury. That, at least, is the legal doctrine. In reality, it often doesn't work out that way. That is because claim interpretation is a matter to be decided by the court, not the jury *(Markman v. Westview Instruments, Inc.,* 517 U.S. 370 Fed. Cir. (1996)). Ultimately, many of these cases turn upon claim interpretation (which also includes an analysis of file history). Both of these topics will be discussed in subsequent chapters.

So, what does the doctrine of equivalents mean in the real world? Remember, an equivalence analysis requires a claim element by claim element analysis. The accused infringing device must be found to contain each and every element of the claim. If the accused infringing device is missing a claim element, then we compare the device to see if that element is found in the accused infringing device to be equivalent to a claim element.

In *Chuiminatta Concrete v. Cardinal Indus.,* 145 F.3d 1303 (Fed. Cir. 1998), the court caused a great deal of alarm in the patent litigation community. That case involved a patent that had a flat metal plate and a saw that protruded from the flat metal plate. The purpose of the saw was to cut concrete, and the purpose of the plate was to hold the concrete in place as the saw cut the concrete. The accused infringing device had a saw, but in place of a flat metal plate it had a hard rubber wheel assembly. As the cutting tool was pushed forward, the hard rubber wheels pushed the cement down and held it in place in the same manner that the flat metal plate did in the preferred embodiment.

The court first held that the particular claim was a means plus function claim. Now, means plus function claim requires its own analysis. A means plus function claim is a claim where the claimed element reads "a means for . . . ." That has traditionally been thought by patent prosecutors to be a broad claim—that is, a means for accomplishing something could involve a number of different structures. The court in *Chuiminatta* held that a means plus function claim is actually an extremely narrow claim. It held that a means plus function term or claim element is limited to the preferred embodiment or its equivalent.

The particular element with which the court was concerned involved "a means for . . . ," which meant essentially holding the concrete down while the saw cut it. The court held that that was a means plus function claim term and therefore was limited to the preferred embodiment or its equivalent. It then analyzed the accused infringing device and said that it clearly did not perform the same function in the same manner to achieve the same result. Its analysis primarily revolved around the structure of the preferred embodiment versus the structure of the accused infringing device. It held that the structure of the preferred embodiment was a flat plate and that the structure of the accused infringing device consisted of a rubber roller. It then held that no reasonable jury could find that a rubber roller and a flat plate performed the same function in essentially the same manner.

Many members of the patent litigation bar were extremely alarmed by this decision. Not only did the court narrow means plus function claim elements, but it also appeared (at least to many lawyers) to be saying that the analysis was really one of structure, and that if the accused infringing device did not have the same structure as the preferred embodiment, then it would not infringe under the doctrine of equivalents.

This decision was viewed by many as an attempt by certain factions on the CAFC to do as much as possible to eliminate the doctrine of equivalents. It is no secret that there are a number of judges on the CAFC who believed (and probably still believe) that the doctrine of equivalents should be eliminated altogether. Their view is that the doctrine of equivalents creates substantial uncertainty as to people's rights to make products without having to be concerned with infringement. The fact that equivalence has been held to be a matter for the trier of fact (read jury) has given that faction further reason to believe that this injected an element of uncertainty. That faction of the court believes that an inventor should be limited to specifically what he sets forth in his disclosure and what is specifically claimed therein.

With that background in mind, many members of the patent litigation bar felt that the narrow holding in *Chuiminatta Concrete* essentially achieved the purpose of eliminating, for all practical purposes, the doctrine of equivalents.

Shortly after the decision in *Chuiminatta Concrete*, however, the court came down with its decision in *Odetics v. Storage Technology Corp.*, 185 F.3d 1259 (Fed. Cir. 1999). In *Odetics*, the court reversed a district court decision in favor of the defendant and held that the doctrine of equivalents does not require that there be equivalent structure, but only that the accused structure meet the means, function, and result test. In doing that analysis, of course, structure can be considered, but there is no requirement that the identical structure or even the "equivalent" structure be found.

Often these cases turn not upon a real analysis of the structure or even the function, manner, and results, but on the manner in which the court interprets the claims and the claim term elements. As a practical matter, many cases result in summary judgment simply based upon the court's claim interpretation. In this regard, fear of the erosion of the role of the jury in these cases has proven to be a legitimate concern.

Reverse Doctrine of Equivalents

One of the sillier doctrines to come down the pike is the Reverse Doctrine of Equivalents. Under that doctrine, even if a device contained each and every element of a claim, it does not infringe if it performs the function performed by the patent device in an essentially different way. In discussing that particular doctrine, the CAFC in the case of *Tate Access Floors v. Interface Architectural Res.*, 279 F.3d 1357 (Fed. Cir. 2002), stated, "Not once has this court affirmed a decision finding noninfringement booked on the reverse doctrine of equivalents. And with good reason . . . ."

One can only hope that someday the CAFC will eliminate that doctrine altogether, as it is, frankly, senseless.

13

Claim Interpretation

So, what does all this mean in terms of claim interpretation? At the risk of being redundant (but these are important concepts), patents are not infringed, specific claims are infringed. At the end of each patent are a number of claims. To determine if there is infringement, an accused infringing product must be compared to the claims, and each and every element found in the claims must be found in the accused infringing product. For example, if a claim consists of "a widget attached by screws to a zaggart," then an accused infringing device must have a widget, it must have a zaggart, and the two must be attached by screws (or their equivalents).

Of Wiggles and Worms

A case I am presently handling involves the terms "wiggle" and "jiggle." The patent in that suit covers a product for dampening vibrations in bowstrings. The preferred embodiment in that patent looks like two worms joined at the center. One worm extends directly to the right and then upward at essentially a 90-degree angle. The second worm extends to the left and downward at essentially a 90-degree angle. According to the preferred embodiment, when the bowstring is released, the upper worm or worm element twists down and the bottom element twists up so that the two worm elements are parallel to each other. The worms also turn, or twist, at their tips. They also oscillate back and forth around the centerpiece, shown by arrows indicating the movement of the various segments. In the written description, it states that the elements of the preferred embodiment bend, oscillate, and otherwise move. It goes on to state that the movement of the invention is shown in the drawings, "and that this wiggling and jiggling . . . ," etc.

The accused infringing device is shaped like a butterfly. It has a central portion that affixes to the string and then two butterfly wings extending on either side. The testimony was that the butterfly wings oscillate back and forth in the manner of a butterfly in flight. The issue is what is meant by the terms or term "wiggle and jiggle." Is "wiggle and jiggle" one term, which is simply a substitute for "bend, oscillate and otherwise move," or does the term "wiggle" have one definition and the term "jiggle" have a different definition?

Defining Terms in Four Steps

In deciding the meaning of a term in a claim, there are essentially four different steps that are taken. The first is to look at the common meaning of the term. If the term has a common, ordinary meaning (which can often be found in the dictionary), then that definition should usually be given. If, however, there are more definitions than one in a dictionary, or different definitions in different dictionaries, then the common and ordinary meaning may not be readily ascertainable.

The second step is to look at the specification of the patent itself to see how the term is defined. If the term does not appear to have a definition that is different from the common, ordinary meaning, then the common, ordinary meaning is the definition that will be given. If there is no common, ordinary meaning or if the definition of the term as shown by the specification is different from the common, ordinary meaning, then the definition set forth in the specification will control.

The court should also look to the file history. The file history documents what representations were made to the Patent Office in the course of attempting to obtain a patent. This also includes making changes to the claims so as to obtain allowance of the patent over the prior art. If statements were made during the prosecution, or if modifications were made to the claims during the prosecution that affect the definition of a term, then the court should consider that as well in determining the meaning of the claim term. Finally, the court can, under limited circumstances, utilize expert testimony.

In *Vitronics v. Conceptronics*, 90 F.3d 1576 (Fed. Cir. 1996), the patentee attempted to use the testimony of an expert to essentially vary the meaning of the claim term from its clear definition as shown by the specification. The court reversed, holding consistent with *Markman v. Westview Instruments, Inc.,* 517 U.S. 370 (1996), that the determination of the meaning of the terms in the claims is the responsibility of the court and, further, that a court may not utilize expert testimony to determine the meaning of a claim term if the meaning of the claim term is clear from the analysis of the factors set forth above. The only time an expert can be utilized is when a claim term has a particular specific meaning known to those in the art. In that type of case, and if the term does not have normal meaning to the average layperson and its meaning is not specifically defined in the patent specification, nor is the file history particularly helpful, then the court may rely upon an expert in defining a claim term. Under no circumstances can a patentee use an expert to vary the clear meaning of a term to his advantage.

In my "wiggle and jiggle" worm and butterfly case, the court granted a preliminary injunction holding that the terms "wiggle and jiggle" were essentially broad terms, which encompassed a wide variety of motions. Unfortunately, I represented the butterfly. We have taken that case on appeal and the appeal is presently pending. Our position was that each term in a claim (in this case, the terms "wiggle" and "jiggle") has independent meaning and must be defined independently. Since the specification showed particular movements that it defined as wiggling and jiggling, and since there was a dictionary definition for wiggle corresponding to one type of motion and a dictionary definition of jiggle corresponding to another type of motion, and since the butterfly device did not move in those directions, then there could be no infringement. We also raised issues of file wrapper estoppel. Because file wrapper estoppel is somewhat complicated, we will give it its own separate chapter, which comes up next.

14

File Wrapper Estoppel

The first thing that any competent patent lawyer defending a party in a patent infringement suit does is to order the "file wrapper" of the patent upon which his client is being sued. The file wrapper is the record kept in the Patent Office of the entire prosecution history of the patent. It consists of the original application and the correspondence between the patent examiner and the lawyer representing the applicant.

Usually, what will be found is a first office rejection of all of the claims by the examiner. The lawyer will then respond, sometimes by amending the claims and sometimes by not amending the claims, but will almost always include "remarks." This process of rejections by the examiner and responses by the lawyer will go back and forth a number of times until finally the patent application receives a final rejection or the application is allowed and the patent issues.

File wrapper estoppel occurs as a result of statements made and amendments made to the claims. The essence of file wrapper estoppel is the same as any kind of estoppel. That is, things that are done and statements that are made can estop a person from taking a contrary position at a later date. In particular, a person is not allowed to, for example, amend the claims to avoid a prior art reference and later assert an interpretation of the claim inconsistent with the amendment. This issue arises under the doctrine of equivalents. For example, if a person has amended the claim to get around a particular prior art reference and in the future wants to argue that an infringing device, which is the same as the prior art reference, infringes under the doctrine of equivalents, the patentee would be estopped from making that argument. Often courts will say that one cannot recapture in litigation what it has given up in prosecution.

Although the classic example of file wrapper estoppel is amending a claim to make the claim more narrow in order to avoid a prior art reference, that is not the only way in which file wrapper estoppel operates. For example, it is my belief (although there are those who may not agree with me and, of course, they would be wrong) that file wrapper estoppel can also be applied to remarks that are made. I once had a case in which, in order to obtain an allowance, the patent lawyer made representations both in writing and in person to the examiner that the patented product would operate in a certain manner when placed in steam. The lawyer used those arguments to distinguish the patented invention (i.e., the claims) from the prior art. While this did not involve a specific amendment to the claims, it did involve a representation as to the manner in which the patented product operated.

In the litigation that ensued, the plaintiff took the position that my client's product infringed even though it operated exactly opposite to the manner in which the patented device operated in a steam environment. We took the position that that constituted file wrapper estoppel, and unfortunately the case was settled while our summary judgment motion was pending; therefore, I did not have the pleasure of seeing my theory lavishly praised by the court.

What happens if the patentee's lawyer makes an amendment to the claims, narrowing them, without doing so in response to any specific prior art or objections raised by the patent examiner?

The Supreme Court, in *Warner Jenkinson Co., Inc. v. Hilton Davis Chemical Co.*, 520 U.S. 17 (1997), held that when such an amendment is made, there is a presumption that it was made for purposes of patentability. In other words, the amendment would bar the application of the doctrine of equivalents to an accused infringing device that would have read upon the claims prior to amendment.

The court did leave open the possibility for the patentee to rebut that presumption and show that there was some reason, other than attempting to obtain the allowance of that claim, for making the amendment. For example, the patentee's lawyer may simply have felt that the amendment was a better means of expressing the claim. The lesson of this is, of course, that it is very dangerous to make narrowing amendments to claims unless it is absolutely necessary to do so, because one may be precluded from asserting the doctrine of equivalents in a case where it might otherwise be totally appropriate.

These waters became further muddied in the case *Festo Corp. v. Shoketsu Kinzoku Kogyo Kabushiki Co.*, 122 S. Ct. 1831 (2002). In that case, the court of appeals held that an amendment made in response to an office action, even if the amendment was not necessarily directed to a particular piece of prior art, would constitute an absolute bar to asserting the doctrine of equivalents for that particular claim element. In its decision, the CAFC referenced *Warner Jenkinson* and said that it was clear that the Supreme Court intended such an absolute bar. It was that reference, to what the CAFC believed the Supreme Court was thinking, that gave rise to the rather caustic remark that I cited earlier when the Supreme Court Justice said that the Court was in a better position to know what it intended than was the CAFC.

The Supreme Court accepted the petition for certiorari and reversed the CAFC, in part. In its reversal, the Court held that while there was a presumption that the amendment was made for patentability, which would absolutely bar the doctrine of equivalents as to the particular claim elements, there is nonetheless an opportunity for rebuttal of that presumption under some circumstances. More often than not, patent prosecutors make these unnecessary amendments for purposes unrelated to patentability—such as, "It just reads better." They then find themselves caught in the presumption.

This is why it is so important for patent prosecutors, and those who hire them, to be very cognizant of what goes on during patent prosecution. Far too often, patent lawyers simply concern themselves with obtaining allowance of a patent without regard to what will happen to that patent once it becomes a trial exhibit.

15

Reissues

Another issue where file wrapper estoppel can come into play involves reissues. I had a case recently where a jury almost gave me a heart attack because it came back in with questions about file wrapper estoppel, which convinced me that the jury was going to find for the defendants and against my client.

What had happened was that during the prosecution of the patent, the lawyer handling the prosecution had made certain representations about the manner in which the invention worked. In the course of doing so, he had attempted to distinguish over the prior art by stating that there were limitations in the manner in which the product functioned. Accordingly, the claims went back to the Patent Office in what is known as a reissue proceeding.

A reissue proceeding is one that must be instituted within a year of the issuance of the patent. Its purpose is to allow the inventor to reshape some of the claims in order to claim something that he had previously neglected to claim but that he was entitled to have claimed in the original patent application. There are a number of restrictions on this kind of proceeding, including the fact that one cannot introduce new disclosure information, nor is one entitled to obtain a patent that is broader than the claims previously contained in the patent as it issued.

In the course of the reissue proceeding, the lawyers handling the proceeding made a number of representations regarding what the invention contained and to what it was directed. They made these representations to obtain the reissue. Incidentally, they also prepared a declaration to be signed by the inventor and then neglected to go over the declaration carefully with him. They submitted the proposed declaration to the president of the company, the president of the company then gave it to the inventor, and the inventor signed it. Unfortunately, the declaration was not discussed in any detail with the inventor, and he said so in his deposition. The lawyers for the defendants then attempted to use this fact as part of their defense of inequitable conduct. We had to have a separate hearing on inequitable conduct (a topic that will be discussed later) and were fortunate that the court did not find inequitable conduct, which would have rendered the patent unenforceable even if it were valid.

In addition to not having gone over the declaration carefully with the inventor, the representations that were made about the scope of the invention, to obtain allowance of the new claim, were, arguably, at odds with some of the language contained in the claims that we were asserting in that litigation. In other words, the file history relating to the reissue could have been construed as being at odds with certain claim interpretations that were necessary to prevent the patent from being held invalid in light of the prior art.

This case was tried shortly before the *Markman* decision came down. Accordingly, there was no decision that said that claim interpretation should be decided by the court. Both sides had argued strenuously about the meaning of different terms in the claims. For some reason, unknown to us at that time and still unknown to us, the court construed certain claims on its own and then, with regard to other terms, merely instructed the jury what our meaning of those terms was and what the other side's meaning of those terms was. The court did not provide an interrogatory to the jury so that jurors could determine what their interpretations of the claims' terms were, but merely instructed the jury to determine whether there was infringement, without any clear demarcation by either the judge or the jury as to the meaning of those controverted terms in the claims.

The jury was out for several days, during which time I had returned home to Mission Viejo. Just as I was preparing to crawl into my nice warm bed, the phone rang and I unwittingly answered it. The call was from my partner, who had stayed behind to answer the jury's questions.

He informed me, in hushed tones, that the jury had asked whether the interpretation of the terms in the claims that we were asserting had to be consistent with the representations made during the reissue proceeding about the scope of the invention. The question was framed along the lines of, "If the invention was intended to have the following characteristics: . . . , then must we find that the term "blah blah" (a made-up term) means the same thing in claims 1 and 2?" Since that particular interpretation of that term in the claims would have meant no infringement, I immediately assumed that the jury was going to enter a judgment against us. Accordingly, I did the only thing that an experienced lawyer would do under the circumstances. I immediately put my clothes back on and prepared to adjourn to the local tavern, where I could drown my sorrows. Just as I was buttoning the last button on my shoes, the phone rang again, at which time my partner informed me that we had prevailed on each and every claim and each and every accused product.[1]

I cite this story not merely to demonstrate infringement and claim interpretation as it relates to file history, but also because it was rather dramatic evidence to me of just how detailed and analytical juries can be when it comes to resolving these cases. The particular concern about the meaning of that particular term in the file history was a matter that had frankly eluded me and had also eluded opposing counsel, who had not made an issue of it at all. The fact is that the jury's question was right on the money and very insightful. This, of course, is the danger in having computer programmers on your jury. Let that be a lesson to all. Beware of the intelligent juror. Seriously, though, this further emphasized to me what I have found over the years, which is that jurors, by and large, are extremely wise, very thoughtful, and usually surprisingly insightful. They also pay a great deal of attention to jury instructions.

This little story also illustrates how important it is that people who prosecute patents be aware of the fact, at all times, that they are preparing a document that is to be used as a trial exhibit and is not to be used merely for the sake of obtaining a patent. I cannot tell you the number of times I have encountered serious problems in litigation that were absolutely and totally unnecessary and were the result of the lawyer handling the patent prosecution not keeping in mind that his or her work product would someday be the subject of intense scrutiny in litigation.

---

1. I still went to the tavern, or "bar," as we refer to them in Mission Viejo. After all, it took me 45 minutes to button my shoes.

16

Anticipation and Obviousness

Now, you may recall that when we were discussing the things you have to have to obtain a patent, we said that the person seeking the patent actually has to be the inventor; that the product cannot have been printed in a publication in a foreign country more than a year before the filing date, nor can it have been made, used, or sold in the United States more than a year before the filing date, unless it was used for experimental purposes.

If the product actually was used publicly in the United States more than a year before the filing date of the application, either by the inventor or by another person, or if the actual invention was described in a prior publication in a foreign country more than a year before the filing date of the application, or if the invention was set forth in a patent that was issued more than a year before the filing date of the application, then the patent sought to be obtained is "held to be anticipated."

Now, as we indicated earlier, these matters are not that simple. Anticipation does not simply mean that the invention was made beforehand but rather that the *particular claims* were invented beforehand. (I'm using the word "beforehand" as shorthand so that I don't have to spell out "a year before . . ." every time.)

Remember, a patent is not defined by the preferred embodiment, that is, the description of the invention in the body of the patent, but rather by the claims. A particular description may support several claims that are variations on the theme. Accordingly, when trying to determine whether a reference anticipates a particular claim, one looks at the reference and attempts to match the claim in question to the disclosure of the prior art. The pithy description of this phenomenon is, "That which infringes if after, anticipates if before."[1] In other words, the way to analyze this is to take the prior art and take the claim and see if the prior art would infringe the claim if the prior art were created after the issuance of the patent. If it would have infringed if it came after the patent issued, then it anticipates if it was created and published, etc., more than a year before the filing date of the invention.

The Patent Search

Accordingly, when the Patent Office is considering whether to issue a patent, an examiner will go to the Patent Office files and attempt to pull out every patent that relates to the subject matter of the patent application. To do a really valid and thorough search, the Patent Office, in addition to seeking to obtain any other information concerning actual products, both in this country and abroad, also should check other publications that may anticipate the proposed invention set forth in the application. As a practical matter, the Patent Office does not have the facilities available to make a complete search. Therefore, one usually will find the Patent Office pulling out primarily United States patent references. Occasionally the Patent Office will cite foreign references as well.

In the real world of patent prosecution, most patents are rejected on a first office action based on prior art available to the Patent Office. Often different claims will be disallowed for different reasons and different prior art, which dramatically points up the fact that each claim is a separate invention, regardless of the fact that they are all based on one preferred embodiment description.

Query: Since the test for anticipation is "that which infringes if after, anticipates if before," how does this relate to the doctrine of equivalents? Remember, the doctrine of equivalents is intended to reach that point wherein the accused product differs slightly from the expressed language of the claims, but the difference is meaningless in terms of invention because the accused device still accomplishes the same objective in the same manner. Does this mean, then, that a prior art reference, which may not read directly on a claim, nonetheless anticipates it if the reference

---

1. As a professor of mine once bellowed to one of my cowering (weren't we all) classmates, "You call that pithy!?"

would anticipate under the doctrine of equivalents? If the reference performs essentially the same function in essentially the same manner to accomplish essentially the same result, is it an anticipatory reference, even though it may not read directly on each and every element of the claim at issue? The answer is no.

A reference that would infringe under the doctrine of equivalents, but that predates the filing of the application by a year, would probably be held to be a reference that might invalidate the patent under the doctrine of obviousness. The doctrine of obviousness says that even though there may not be a reference that anticipates the invention (that is, contains every one of the elements of the claim in question), it may be "obvious" to combine more than one reference to create the invention. (The term "invention" when used in this context always refers to a claim, not to the disclosure or the invention as a whole.)

An Obvious Example

An example of obviousness (which I am conveniently making up) would be an electrical circuit that includes as one of the elements a rheostat as a light switch. A prior art reference shows exactly the same circuitry, only without the use of a rheostat as the light switch.[2] While the particular prior art reference does not show the use of a rheostat, many of the references do show a rheostat as a particular light switch that can be used in virtually any circuit. Accordingly, the examiner would find that it would be obvious to use a rheostat in place of a regular light switch and therefore would deny the invention, on the basis that there is no inventive novelty in using a circuit that was previously invented and published, making only the insignificant modification of using a rheostat instead of a regular light switch.

The particular example that I have just presented is a very simple one and would be a no-brainer for the Patent Office. Obviously, most cases are a lot closer than the example I have just given. More often than not, an examiner will, in the first office action, throw every patent that has any one of the claimed features of the invention into the hopper and claim that the invention is obvious, because it would be obvious to anyone "skilled in the art" to combine all of the different references. That's when the business of the patent prosecution begins.

After the usual rejection on the basis of obviousness, there will be a

---

2. A rheostat, in case you are not familiar with the term, is a dimmer switch.

number of communications between the patent lawyer and the examiner wherein claims will be modified and arguments will be presented about why it is not obvious to combine different references to reach the result of the invention. Whether these efforts are successful will determine whether the patent issues and, if so, what will be the exact wording of those claims that will issue in the patent. It is this question of "obviousness" that is one of the areas of greatest controversy in patent law.

Clearly, there is a certain amount of subjective analysis in making that determination. In the example that I gave above, it is obvious to interchange different types of switches. Where obviousness becomes more subtle and difficult is particularly in the area where more than two references are combined.

Now that you understand the concepts, differences, and similarities between anticipatory references and obviousness references, it might seem that these are basically degrees of the same thing. Something that is extremely obvious might be said to be so obvious that it anticipates. That, of course, is not true. *Anticipation means each and every claim element is found in one reference. Obviousness requires combining references.*

Case Findings

Be prepared for one of the many strange quirks in patent law. The question of whether a reference anticipates, in litigation, is a question of fact for the jury. *Hazani v. U.S. International Trade Commission*, 126 F.3d 1473, 1477 (Fed. Cir. 1997). *In re Graves*, 69 F.3d 1147, 1152 (Fed. Cir. 1995) (A reference anticipates a patent claim if it discloses the claimed invention "such that a skilled artisan could take its teachings in combination with his own knowledge of the particular art and be in possession of the invention."). *American Hoist & Derrick Co. v. Sowa & Sons*, 725 F.2d 1350, 1359-60 (Fed. Cir. 1984).

The question of whether the patent is *obvious*, and therefore invalid, in light of prior art references is *not a question of fact*, but is a question of *law for the court*. Obviousness under 35 U.S.C. § 103 is a legal conclusion involving four factual inquiries. *B.F. Goodrich Co. v. Aircraft Braking Systems Corp.*, 72 F.3d 1577, 1582 (Fed. Cir. 1996).

When obviousness is based on a particular prior art reference, there must be a showing of a suggestion or motivation to modify the teachings of that reference. *Id.* The test is what the combined teachings of the references would have suggested to those of ordinary skill in the art. *Cable Electric Products, Inc. v. Genmark, Inc.*, 770 F.2d 1015, 1025 (Fed. Cir.

1985); *In re* Keller, 642 F.2d 413, 425 (Fed. Cir. 1981). It is only necessary that one of ordinary skill in the art apply "knowledge clearly present
in the prior art." *In re* Sernaker, 702 F.2d 989, 995 (Fed. Cir. 1983).
Inherency also arises in the context of obviousness. *In re* Napier, 55 F.3d
610, 613 (Fed. Cir. 1995).

In re Borcherdt, 197 F.2d 550, 551 (C.C.P.A. 1952); *In re* LaVerne,
229 F.2d 470, 474 (C.C.P.A. 1956); *In re* Switzer, 166 F.2d 827, 831
(C.C.P.A. 1948); *South Corp. v. United States,* 690 F. 1368, 1369 (Fed.
Cir. 1982); *Plastic Container Corp. v. Continental Plastics*, 515 F. Supp.
834, 851 (W.D. Okla. 1980) ("Where, as here, a particular limitation in a
claim (the thumb pushing function) is the only basis upon which the
claim was allowed, the disclosure of the same feature and limitation in
prior art not cited by the Patent Office renders the claim invalid under 35
U.S.C. § 103."); *Ashland Oil, Inc. v. Delta Resins and Refractories, Inc.
*, 776 F.2d 281, 291-92 (Fed. Cir. 1985).

Ryko Mfg. Co. v. Nu-Star, Inc., 950 F.2d 714, 719 (Fed. Cir. 1991),
citing *Newell Companies, Inc. v. Kenney Mfg. Co.*, 864 F.2d 757, 768
(Fed. Cir. 1988).

Accordingly, if a jury should determine that a reference is anticipatory and invalidates the patent, this would *not* be subject to de novo review by the Court of Appeals for the Federal Circuit. On the other hand,
should the court find that a patent is obvious in light of prior art references, this is a determination of law and *is* subject to de novo review by
the CAFC.

Now, be prepared for the next anomaly—it ain't so.

Even though, as a technical matter, issues of obviousness are matters
of law for the court, they are usually tried to the jury. Of course, a trial
court theoretically has the option of disregarding the jury's finding on
obviousness and substituting its own.

As a practical matter, the court simply refers this matter to the jury in
the form of an interrogatory and then adopts the jury's finding as its own.
This, of course, is a procedure often followed by trial courts when they
are trying cases in equity. Whether the determination of obviousness is
made by a judge or by a jury and thereafter adopted by the judge, the
courts of appeals do not usually treat determinations of obviousness as
strictly issues of law for their own determination. The CAFC uses phrases
that indicate that it is giving great deference to the analysis of the trier of
fact, be it judge or jury.

Now that you understand what anticipation and obviousness are and
who decides what in a trial, let's discuss the difference between how
these issues are handled in the Patent Office and how they are handled in
litigation, particularly during discovery.

As I indicated above, when the patent examiner receives a new application, the examiner conducts a search of the Patent Office files to see if he or she can locate any previously issued patents, in the United States or sometimes abroad, that either anticipate the invention or are references that, if combined, would produce the invention, and if it would be obvious to combine them. There are two problems with this system. The first is that examiners generally have limited resources. That means that the examiner will probably not have access to magazines, books, transcripts of speeches and presentations, service manuals, etc. Remember, for purposes of prior art, any printed publication or any use in the United States more than one year before the filing of the application constitutes prior art. So the patent examiner will often miss a number of critical pieces of prior art.

Now, not surprisingly, in litigation, greater weight is given to the question of obviousness to prior art that was not considered by the Patent Office. The standard phrase presented to the jury in closing argument is, "If the examiner had this information in front of him, this patent would never have issued." On the other hand, one can still raise the issue of whether the patent examiner correctly analyzed the prior art that was presented to him or her. The reason this can be done at trial is because of the second problem with the patent prosecution process, which is that it is ex parte. In other words, the examiner is hearing only from the lawyer who wants the patent to issue, and is receiving no input from those who may believe that the patent should not issue. Often examiners, who are under a time constraint, will accept arguments presented by a patentee's lawyer that never should have been accepted.

Of course, the patent is presumed to be valid, and this presumption has to be overcome in court; and it is often a very difficult one to overcome, even if the facts might appear to justify it. This is due not only to the fact of the legal presumption but also to the psychological barrier that must be overcome with juries, most of whom have a fair amount of respect for that fancy document with the ribboned seal. There is a procedure whereby a person who believes that a patent should not have issued can have the patent reconsidered by the Patent Office. That procedure is known as reexamination. (We will discuss this issue separately in its own chapter.)

It is because the Patent Office searches are limited that a lawyer whose client is being sued for patent infringement should not assume the patent is valid, but should begin an intensive prior art search. This usually is done and, as discussed in the section on discovery, is often very expensive and can extend worldwide. I usually advise my clients that the best place to start a prior art search is within their own industry. I find that most of the clients I represent have research and development and sales personnel who are far more attuned to the state of the art in that particular industry than any patent examiner or patent lawyer could be.

Incidentally, the general rule is that any lawyer dealing with a potential patent application or patent infringement suit should engage in the most extensive worldwide search possible. A lawyer considering the filing of a patent application for a client does the client small service if that lawyer fails to find pertinent prior art that later invalidates the patent.

The same caveat should be taken into consideration when determining whether to purchase patents or take a license on patents.

My general approach to the whole subject of patents is to treat all patents, whether they are at the stage of applying for a patent or of acquiring the patent, suing on a patent or defending on a patent, as though the invention were being challenged in court. When asked to give an opinion on the validity of a patent, I approach the issue as though I were in court. I make every attempt to overturn every stone to find every piece of prior art that may be even peripherally relevant to the subject invention.

Unfortunately, many lawyers will file an application for a patent or okay the acquisition of patent rights without having vigorously attacked the potential validity of the patent. Some lawyers will even file an application on a patent without having done a preliminary search of the Patent Office. This, in my opinion, is a grievous error and may even be close to malpractice.

Also bear in mind that the inventor and the inventor's lawyer have an obligation to inform the Patent Office of any prior art of which they are aware that may be relevant to the validity of the patent for which application is being made. To not make even a preliminary inquiry as to the state of the prior art seems to me to skirt very close to violating this requirement.

The Tilton Case

Going back to the subject of anticipation and obviousness issues in litigation, it might be helpful if I recited a couple of my own experiences.

In the *Tilton* case, to which we have alluded previously, our client was the inventor of the carbon/carbon clutch. It was called a carbon/carbon clutch because the material being utilized was carbon impregnated with carbon in a matrix that provided unusual strength. The particular carbon/carbon materials were not invented by the client but had been developed for use in the Stealth bomber and other Stealth aircraft that utilized that particular material for brakes. Because the carbon/carbon material had strength characteristics comparable to steel, yet at a fraction of the weight of steel (weight being determined in terms of torque necessary to turn the metal or carbon/carbon disc), there were tremendous potential power advantages to the use of the carbon/carbon material in clutches as opposed to the use of the standard steel discs that one finds in the standard clutch.

Tilton's opponent in that particular litigation, Automotive Products, had engaged in extensive experiments in attempting to develop a clutch using the carbon/carbon material. All of its efforts had failed. Subsequently, one of Automotive Products' employees moved from England to the United States and went to work for Tilton Engineering. While at Tilton Engineering, he and Mac Tilton and others came up with an idea that would solve the fundamental problem that had been encountered in attempting to utilize this material. The problem was that positioning the carbon discs in the center of the clutch required affixing them somehow to the metal hub. The technique that all the parties had been attempting up to that time was to rivet the carbon/carbon clutch disc to a steel plate. But while the carbon/carbon material had tremendous strength in certain directions, it lacked it in others. As far as a screw was concerned, it was almost like trying to screw a piece of brittle plastic or even glass to a metal plate. As soon as the disc began any kind of circular motion, it would shear off the pins that were affixing it to the metal hub.

The solution developed by Tilton was to avoid the necessity of permanently affixing the hub to a metal plate by using an alternative design that was so simple it is frankly embarrassing. (Most great inventions involve some seemingly simplistic answers to a problem. Of course, it's simple once someone else thinks of it.) Rather than bolt, rivet, or screw the discs to a metal hub, they simply cut slots in the disc and fashioned a hub with ribs so that the disc could slide over the ribs and sit there without being permanently attached. This was known as the "floating hub" design. When the clutch was engaged, the spring mechanism would force the metal and carbon plates together in a tight fit so that it operated in the same fashion as a standard clutch. When the clutch was disengaged, the separation of the clutch discs from the center carbon disc would allow the carbon disc to float freely on the hub without sliding off. This was an ingenious solution to a seemingly intractable problem that merely required standing back from the problem and looking at it from a slightly different angle. It is this kind of "spark" that makes an invention an invention.

In the prosecution of the patent, there were no patents found that involved the use of the carbon/carbon material for a clutch. Most of the prior art that was considered by the Patent Office involved the use of carbon/carbon materials in aircraft brakes. When the case got to trial, the defendant (actually, it was the counterdefendant, since the suit had been instituted initially by Automotive Products seeking to have Tilton's patent declared invalid—a declaratory judgment action), Automotive Products, relied heavily on the aircraft brake industry as its prior art. It even brought in a huge aircraft brake drum and paraded it throughout the courtroom. The drum was a big old rusted monstrosity, but it demonstrated the technology that AP wanted to assert. I believe, without knowing for a fact, that the mere disparity of the size and the type of use between that monstrosity and the tiny little compact clutch manufactured by Tilton had an impact on the jury. In my experience, juries react very strongly to things that they can touch, see, feel, and hear. When you are comparing a huge airplane brake with a small automobile clutch and are saying that they are same thing, this is bound to have a negative impact on most jurors.

At that point in time, we were feeling pretty comfortable about our case. Our comfort level was further increased by the fact that one of AP's prime experts, a professor from Cal Tech, admitted that he had absolutely no hands-on experience in dealing with clutches, which prompted the judge to ask him, in the presence of the jury, how he could be an expert on clutches. Nonetheless, the judge allowed him to testify as an expert because of his general engineering background and the fact that he was a professor of engineering.[3] Nonetheless, you could see the psychological impact that his lack of experience with clutches had on the jury.

Just when I was feeling quite comfortable with our case, I was jolted out of my pastoral torpor by another of AP's experts, who produced a motorcycle clutch that had (gasp) a floating hub. When we recessed for the day, I went over and grabbed that exhibit, lifted it to my eyes, took it apart, and could not believe what I was seeing. But for the fact that it used metal pieces (no carbon was to be found anywhere), it appeared to be almost identical to our client's design. The key to our client's invention consisted not of the floating hub design alone but of the utilization of a floating hub design in conjunction with a particular material. There were also structural differences between the motorcycle clutch with the floating hub and my client's carbon/carbon floating hub clutch.

Now the question is, "Would my client have been better off if the Patent Office had known about that particular motorcycle clutch before deciding whether or not to issue the patent?" There are a number of ways of looking at that issue. The first, of course, is that had the lawyer

---

3. This in spite of the fact that he *admitted under oath* that he taught at Cal Tech.

(in this particular case it was a patent agent) known about that clutch, he would have had an obligation to inform the Patent Office because it was clearly relevant. He was not aware of it, nor were we aware of it until after the case was well in progress.[4]

Had the Patent Office been aware of that clutch, there is, of course, the very real possibility that it would have denied the patent on the basis that it would be obvious to combine a carbon disc such as the type used in the airline brake drums with a floating hub arrangement such as was found in that particular motorcycle clutch. On the other hand, if the Patent Office had known about that clutch and issued the patent anyway, it would have shielded AP from the accused infringer's being able to say, "Had the Patent Office known about this clutch, it never would have issued the patent in the first place." While it may seem that the issue was moot in that particular case because the Patent Office didn't know of the clutch, and therefore the arguments were going to play out regardless, that issue often arises where the reexamination procedure is concerned.

---

4. You are probably saying "So, if you're such a great lawyer, why didn't you find out about it before trial?" The answer is—I'm obviously not such a great lawyer.

17

Prior Public Use

A doctrine to which we alluded previously was that regarding prior public use versus experimental use. Under the public use doctrine, a person who has used her invention or publicly displayed or sold the invention more than a year prior to the filing of the application loses her right to file for a patent. An exception is where the use was done strictly for experimental purposes, which avoids the one-year bar.[1]

In *Beachcombers v. Wildwood*, which we discussed earlier, we had a rather unusual situation. There were no prior publications demonstrating or illustrating the device patented by the plaintiff that was sought to be enforced against my client. Also, the plaintiff, the patent holder, had not made, used, or sold his invention more than a year before filing the application. He claimed to have invented his application years before filing it, which gave rise to another defense—that he had waived his rights by sleeping on them. (No, not literally. This defense of sleeping on one's rights is a sort of estoppel defense and is very difficult to maintain. It was the only defense that we lost in that case, but we didn't need it anyway.)

Since there were no prior publications and the inventor had not made, used, or sold his invention more than a year before the filing of the appli-

---

1. The public use bar to a U.S. patent does not apply to public use in foreign countries. In most foreign countries, public use or sale anywhere in the world, before filing a patent application, will void patent rights. These rights can be preserved in most countries by a U.S. filing prior to use or sale. Consult your patent lawyer; don't try this at home.

cation, how come we were able to have his patent declared invalid on the basis of anticipation? The answer is in that case, someone else had invented the identical device and had shown it at a party of her friends and friends of friends (i.e., an open party) one year and two months before the filing date of the plaintiff's patent application.

As I said before, usually it is the inventor who has made, used, or sold the invention and who argues that it was never intended for anyone in the public domain to know about it. In fact, one of the leading cases involves an inventor who showed off his invention at a party of friends and thereafter argued that it was never intended for public dissemination because this was just a close-knit group of friends, and he never intended or expected that they would tell anyone else about the invention.

In our case, we had just the opposite. The plaintiff's lawyers tried desperately, on cross-examination, to attempt to force the other inventor to state that she never intended her invention to be disseminated to the public. She had nothing to gain one way or the other (so she was a very credible witness), and her uncontroverted testimony was that not only did she not intend to keep her invention confidential, but one of the reasons she had the kind of party she had was so that she could get feedback from people about what they thought of the commercial viability of her kaleidoscopes. She also testified that her parties were open to others, and she encouraged people to go out and talk about the qualities and characteristics of her new kaleidoscopes.

The plaintiff's lawyers were quite dissatisfied with her version of things and cross-examined her for an entire day, getting nowhere. At the end of the day the poor woman was in tears, and the jurors were throwing looks of undisguised disdain at the plaintiff's lawyer's desperate efforts.

On appeal, the plaintiff's lawyers argued that she should not have been believed, that in spite of her uncontroverted testimony she really intended for her product to be kept a deep, dark secret. Plaintiff's lawyers also argued that there were no cases of record (at least none they could find) in which prior public use by one other than the patent holder would render another person's patent invalid. Of course, her prior public use of the invention that contained the exact elements of the plaintiff's invention was prior public use, and therefore prior art in the public domain, more than a year before the filing date of the application, which rendered the patent invalid.

The jury also found the patent invalid because it was obvious, and additionally found that it was not infringed. As one of the jurors said to me afterward, "I think he thinks he invented something, but I am not sure what it was, and it certainly wasn't what was in his patent."

Incidentally, that was a case in which I moved for summary judgment and it was denied. That raises an interesting question in and of itself. Since the prior art was anticipatory, arguably that was a question of fact for the jury and not an appropriate determination for the court. If, on the other hand, the prior art had been very close, and there had been another piece of prior art that, when combined with the first piece of prior art, would constitute the invention, then that probably would have been an appropriate subject matter for summary judgment, since obviousness, unlike anticipation, is a question of law for the court. Finally, since infringement is a question of fact and not law, infringement was an issue of fact for the jury. This case seemed to me to demonstrate once again the intellectual inconsistency between saying that anticipation should be an issue of fact, whereas obviousness should be an issue of law, and infringement should be an issue of fact.

18

Reexamination

Until a few years ago, if a patent was issued, the only way that a person could raise the issue of the validity of that patent was in a federal district court. In other words, the only way that a patent could be determined to be valid was either by an ex parte proceeding, where no one was heard from the other side, or in a full-blown judicial process. To provide some sort of intermediate approach, the Patent Office (actually, it was probably Congress) developed a proceeding called "reexamination."

Under the reexamination procedure, a person, either the inventor or someone challenging the patent, can seek to have the issued patent reexamined to determine if it should have issued in the first place or if it should reissue with modifications. The criteria for determining whether there should be a reexamination are: (a) whether there is art that was not considered by the Patent Office in the original proceedings; and (b) which art is relevant to the question of anticipation or obviousness.

When the proceeding is instituted by a third party, it is a semi-contested proceeding. The procedure is that the person contesting the patent files a petition seeking reexamination. In that petition, the person will lay out the art not considered by the Patent Office and the reasons why that art should render the patent invalid. The person who has obtained the patent then has the right to respond, and thereafter the proceeding becomes ex parte. In other words, the person who originally sought reexamination steps out of the picture, and the Patent Office then determines whether to grant the request for reexamination. If the Patent Office grants the request for reexamination, it thereafter communicates directly with the patent holder, and there is no further input from the person who sought reexamination in the first instance.

Now, you may have noticed that I said in a situation where a person challenging the patent seeks reexamination, it is a semi-ex parte proceeding. Some of you (who are brighter than the others) may be asking yourselves, "Who else other than a person seeking to have the patent set aside would seek reexamination?" The answer is, the inventor may seek reexamination. "Why?" you ask incredulously.

Perhaps your inventor (your client) had you send letters to a bunch of people who your client felt were infringing her patent. Feeling unusually aggressive and not having the patience or the tolerance to deal with a patent lawyer on that particular day, you sent out a score of scathing missives accusing all of your client's competitors of willfully, viciously, and horrendously infringing your client's breakthrough patent on automated ringless widgets.

For all your trouble, you receive a snowstorm of scathing replies from a bunch of fat lawyers with nothing else to do but send you brochures, patents, advertisements, sketches, drawings, schematics, and photographs of billboards of devices containing all the features of your client's ringless widget, all of which were in the public domain five to 25 years before your client ever put pen to paper.[1]

"Well," you say. "What should I do now? I know, I'll just sue these people anyway. I'll get a patent infringement complaint out of this book I'm reading; I'll fill in the blanks, and I'll let those guys worry about all that prior art they think is so important." Is this the correct approach? Yes, it is. OK, maybe it isn't. Then again, maybe it is. As my evidence teacher use to say, "These are tough questions."

Before running off and filing a complaint, however, you review this chapter in this book and you also call your local patent lawyer friend. (Actually, patent lawyers have no friends, so to be perfectly accurate we should say your patent lawyer acquaintance.) You say to yourself, "I heard somewhere, or remember someone saying, or I believe my mother told me long ago, 'There is a provision in the patent laws that says that if my case has no merit, my client can be hit for sanctions.'" There is also a provision in the federal rules called Rule 11, which says the lawyer can be hit for sanctions. This is scary stuff indeed.

---

1. Or, if your client was a "dot.com" whiz-kid, 10 years before he cost you your life savings. How could so many wet-behind-the-ears kids bamboozle so many of us?

You begin thinking about your client's options. Here the client has a perfectly valid U.S. patent with a nice seal and ribbon on it that says so. She also has a nasty group of infringers who, at least arguably, are producing products that read on the client's claim either directly or under the doctrine of equivalents. Nonetheless, you are now aware of the fact that there is prior art, never considered by the Patent Office, that might theoretically invalidate your client's patent. What are your choices? Well, under the old scheme, your only choice was either forget about it or file a lawsuit. Sometimes this decision would be made for you, because the other side would file an action to have your patent declared invalid.

Under the new reexamination procedures, your client can challenge her own patent. You can make the Patent Office aware of the fact that new art has been found that you believe the Patent Office should consider in determining whether to keep the patent as it was or perhaps allow it to go forward but with some amended and narrower claims. The disadvantage of this procedure, of course, is that the Patent Office may take you up on your offer and may throw out your client's patent. On the other hand, if the Patent Office considers the prior art that you have presented to it and still allows your patent to issue, then you have a much stronger patent. What often happens is that the Patent Office will work a deal with the inventor in which the inventor might drop some of her broader claims but the Patent Office still allows some of the narrower claims to exist in the patent. This may mean that the inventor may not be able to sue as many people as she might like; on the other hand, it means that whoever she sues will have a much greater likelihood of being sued successfully.

In patent law, as in most fields of the law, negotiations play a large part, and often, when an inventor or the owner of a patent can emerge from reexamination with the patent intact, this strengthens the bargaining arm considerably.

Sanctions can be granted if the case is found to be an exceptional case, which usually means willful infringement of a valid patent. If all those people who wrote you the scathing letters now receive a letter back from you saying, "Aha! We took the prior art that you gave us seriously; we submitted it to the Patent Office, and guess what, the Patent Office considered all that stuff and reissued the patent anyway, and you still infringe."

Accused infringers who receive a letter like that and become aware of the fact that their products read on the claims[2] (at least, the ones that

---

2. That is, each and every element of a claim is found in the product accused of infringing that particular claim.

are left) of your patent run a very serious risk of being nailed for willful infringement if they ignore the fact that your patent has reissued over the art that they cited to you. By the same token, an accused infringer, in deciding whether to seek reexamination of another's patent, has to take into consideration the fact that the patent he is accused of infringing may emerge that much stronger from reexamination, and thereby weaken the infringer's chances of defending in court.

In other words, the reexamination proceeding is a useful one, but one that must be carefully considered as one of many options for both patentees and accused potential infringers.

In the *Tilton* case that we have been using as an example, Automotive Products did seek reexamination of Tilton's patent, based on what its patent lawyers in Detroit considered to be prior art. Not only did it not succeed in having the patent set aside, but the Patent Office refused even to grant the petition for reconsideration. This substantially strengthened Tilton's hand at trial, and we were able to argue that there was increased presumption of validity based on the fact that the Patent Office would not even grant reexamination. This was an example where an attempt to have someone else's patent thrown out by the Patent Office through a reexamination proceeding backfired and strengthened the hand of the patent holder.

19

Inequitable Conduct

The Court of Appeals for the Federal Circuit has referred to allegations of inequitable conduct as a "plague" on the courts. This characterization is not far from the mark, and you would think that, given that kind of scornful evaluation of the defense of inequitable conduct, lawyers would scurry away from that defense like cockroaches from a halogen light. Au contraire, mon frère. It is just the opposite. For some reason it appears that an allegation of inequitable conduct (which is actually fraud on the Patent Office) rears its ugly head in virtually every patent infringement case.

The boilerplate charge of inequitable conduct is failure to bring to the attention of the Patent Office prior art of which the inventor or his lawyer was aware and which would have been relevant to a reasonable examiner in making a determination of whether the patent should issue. There are two requirements regarding inequitable conduct. The first is that the conduct must be willful, and the second is that the conduct must be material. Materiality means that it would have been important to a reasonable examiner in determining whether the patent should issue.

One reason that inequitable conduct is so often raised as a defense is that there is almost no such thing as a perfect patent prosecution. One can almost always find prior art that was not presented to the Patent Office because hardly anyone is able to conduct a perfect prior art search. It is not at all unusual for the lawyer prosecuting the patent to look at various pieces of prior art and conclude that they are not particularly relevant or not as relevant as prior art that the lawyer has already cited to the Patent Office or that the Patent Office has discovered on its own.

Also, there are many instances where a lawyer would argue about the particular meaning or significance of a piece of prior art to the examiner. Once in litigation, the lawyer for the defendant will argue that the representations concerning the prior art made by the lawyer for the patentee were misleading and intentionally misleading to the examiner, who was seduced by the wily and artful arguments of the smooth-talking patent lawyer. (Yeah, right.)

In a case that I recently tried, the patentee (whom I represented as plaintiff) had obtained a new claim during a reissue proceeding. A reissue proceeding is one in which the patentee, within two years of obtaining the patent, goes back to the Patent Office and says that he was entitled to claim something in addition to (i.e., broader than) that which he had claimed previously. (This is not the only reissue proceeding, but the others aren't that dramatic.)

One of the reasons people seek to obtain reissue patents is because sometimes they discover that a third party is making a product that does not infringe any of the claims in the patent, but would nonetheless have infringed claims in the patent to which the patentee would have been entitled if those claims had existed in the patent in the first instance. To correct this perceived injustice, the patentee goes back to the Patent Office and obtains a new claim or claims that cover the patented product.

Since the question of what is an appropriate claim, how to word a claim, and whether a claim is broad or narrow is a matter within the technical expertise of the lawyer, these petitions for reexamination are almost always prepared by the lawyer, even though the supporting declarations are signed by the patentee. This points up a constant problem in patent law, which is that there is a dichotomy between the expertise of the lawyer, who is responsible for preparing and prosecuting the patent, and the expertise of the inventor, who is usually better versed in the technology of the invention than the lawyer.

In this particular case, the lawyer prepared the declaration and petition for reexamination and gave them to the president of the company, who in turn gave the declaration to the inventor for his signature. The whole thing was Greek to the inventor, who just signed it without reading or understanding it. He then gave it back to the president, who gave it back to the lawyers, who in turn filed it with the Patent Office.

During the inventor's deposition, he correctly and truthfully answered that he had not carefully read and certainly did not understand the declaration in support of the petition to reissue that he had signed. The defendants latched on to this succulent piece of information like gum on a grate. As far as they were concerned, this was the most egregious case of blatant inequitable conduct and fraud on the Patent Office they had ever seen. They were aghast with mock horror at the spectacle of an inventor actually signing a declaration about broad and narrow claims without first having a firm foundation and understanding of patent law. In addition, the defendant took the position that even though the lawyers were saying that the new proposed claim was narrower than the previous allowed claims, in fact it was broader, and this was further evidence of willful and deliberate fraud by the lawyers.

This was a relatively novel theory, since normally one assumes that the patent examiner can tell the difference between broad and narrow claims, regardless of how the lawyer characterizes them. Inequitable conduct normally is reserved for situations where information is withheld from the examiner or material misrepresentations (such as false statements about the nature of the product) are made to the examiner, and the examiner has no ability to make an independent determination about the misinformation. This concern is a direct result of the fact that patent prosecution is ex parte, and the patent examiner must rely to a large extent on representations of facts, unknowable to the examiner, which are made by the applicant or the applicant's lawyer.

As a result of the defendant's lawyer having acquired this brand-new and powerful ammunition, the court had a special pretrial hearing with witnesses and evidence and endless arguments of counsel to determine whether there was in fact inequitable conduct. At the close of the hearing, six months later, the court found no inequitable conduct and cleared the way for a trial on the merits.

In another case in which I was not so fortunate (or I should say my client was not so fortunate), my client was in the business of making a product that it had patented with a method and equipment that also were patented. The product had been developed over a substantial period of time (a number of years). The starting point for the development of the product was with a patented process and product to which my client had purchased the rights.

When the teachings of the patent were followed, the product that was produced was simply not suitable for commercial purposes. Over the years, my client had developed a number of improvements in both the equipment and method of manufacturing the product and in the product itself. Finally, the client perfected the process and obtained the high-quality product that became the backbone of the company.

In the course of the development of the various stages of the process, equipment, and product, my client kept a series of laboratory notebooks. These notebooks contained information concerning the evolution of the process, equipment, and product throughout the various stages. (Theoretically, this is a sound principle and one that all of you should encourage the people in your clients' research and development departments to follow.) The client then retained the services of a patent lawyer, who filed an application and began the process of prosecuting or attempting to obtain a patent. (Actually, there were three patents as a result of continuations in part and divisional applications.)

My client actually sold some of the product made with the intermediate equipment and processes before perfecting the invention that eventually became the patented process, equipment, and product. These products had been sold more than a year before the filing of the application.

Having perfected the process, equipment, and product, my client gave a patent lawyer the information that he needed to prepare the application.

During the trial, the original lawyer testified that he had not been told that my client had commercially sold intermediate product. This was contrary to the testimony of the inventor, who claimed that he had in fact given the lawyer this information. In any event—and this was crucial to the case—the original patent lawyer testified as to how he defined prior art when he advised the inventor. (As you may recall, prior art must be disclosed to the Patent Office if the inventor is aware of it.) In this case, the lawyer testified that he had told his client that prior art consisted of patents, publications, or the actual invention itself. He also advised the inventor that if he had made, used, or sold the invention more than a year before the filing of the application, he could not file it. He never testified that he advised his client that prior art also would include intermediate products, not made in accordance with the teaching of the invention, that also were sold more than a year prior to the filing date.

As a result, the Patent Office was never told about the sale of the intermediate product. This was one of the grounds asserted by the defendants as inequitable conduct by my client. The court agreed with the defendants and found in an order (prepared by the defendants pursuant to the court's instruction) that my client had willfully concealed the information about these intermediate product sales from the Patent Office.

The issue on appeal (which is still pending) is, how could the court have found that my client (the court did not find that the lawyer did anything wrong) willfully concealed the prior art from the Patent Office when there was no evidence that my client was ever even told that this intermediate product was in fact prior art? (This is a consideration separate from the fact that my client testified that it did inform the patent lawyer about the intermediate products.) In addition, all of the intermediate methods, products, and equipment were discussed in the patent as product that was made by the inventor and was distinguished from the product, process, and equipment of the patent itself. In other words, there was disclosure of this prior art in the patent. The only thing that was not done was that the examiner was never specifically told that there were sales of intermediate product. The issue on appeal, therefore, is squarely one of intent, and since intent must be proven by direct evidence (it cannot simply be inferred by the fact that there was information given or withheld), I feel comfortable that we will prevail on this issue on appeal. You, the reader, will simply have to wait for the supplement to this book to find out.

This was not the only inequitable conduct issue raised in that case. There were two additional issues. The first of the two remaining issues related to abandonment. Sometime during the course of the prosecution of the patent, my client decided to change patent lawyers. Before switching lawyers, it had received a rejection of the patent from the Patent Office that required a response within a certain given period of time or else the patent would go abandoned. Because the client had decided to obtain the services of another patent lawyer, it directed that the first lawyer cease his efforts. The first lawyer had in fact written to my client and informed it of the deadlines for responses and that if these deadlines were not met, the patent would go abandoned. This communication was delivered to an officer of the company, but not to the inventor. In the meantime, the inventor was seeking the services of another lawyer and was not aware of the deadline.

The services of a new lawyer were obtained, but not until after the deadline for filing a response had already expired, and, accordingly, the patent went abandoned. Under the rules of procedure of the Patent Office, an abandoned application can be revived within one year of abandonment if the abandonment was not intentional. Accordingly, the new lawyer prepared a form declaration for signature by the inventor stating that he had not intentionally abandoned the application. This form, with the requisite fee (there is always a fee), was filed, and the petition to revive the application was granted.

At the hearing, the defendants argued that the abandonment was intentional because the inventor was informed of the deadline but did not secure the services of the new lawyer before the deadline, and because the inventor told the first lawyer to cease his efforts. The first lawyer was called in to testify, and he refused (in spite of the persistent efforts of the defendants' counsel) to state that my client ever told him that it intended to abandon the application. He did acknowledge (and this fact was not controverted) that he was personally told to stop working on it. His testimony was that this could have meant either that the client intended to abandon it or that it merely intended to secure the services of another lawyer, and that was a matter for the court to decide.

Unfortunately for my client, the court concluded that the abandonment was intentional. The court made this decision in spite of the fact that the inventor, the president of the company, and the lawyer who took over the prosecution of the patent all testified that there was never an intention to abandon the application. The court simply chose to not believe the testimony of my client and my witnesses.

The issue for appeal on that finding again goes to the question of intention as well as the issue of whether a court can disbelieve the uncontroverted testimony of witnesses. It was our position (and I firmly believe we are correct) that a court may not simply disregard the uncontroverted testimony of witnesses unless a reason is given. We cited two Ninth Circuit cases in which there actually was a reversal of a judicial decision because the judges chose to disregard uncontroverted testimony and failed to give any reasons for why the testimony was disregarded.

The second remaining issue was a little more complicated.

If you recall, we indicated earlier that prior art can include foreign publications. Once the prosecution of the patent had resumed under the direction of the new lawyer, the patent examiner found a Japanese patent that he cited against my client as prior art that would have invalidated certain claims because the Japanese patent was published before the filing date of the application. The question then became, did the U.S. inventor actually invent before the Japanese inventor? Since the Japanese patent issued before the U.S. inventor (my client) filed his application, the U.S. inventor had to show that his invention was actually made (reduced to practice) at least before the publication date of the Japanese patent. This was the only way to eliminate the Japanese patent as prior art.

The patent lawyer went back to my client and asked if it had actually reduced the invention to practice before the publication date of the Japanese reference. Also, if there was a conception of the invention before the publication date and due diligence thereafter in reducing it to practice, that could still suffice to get behind the Japanese reference, even if the actual reduction to practice did not occur until after the publication date of the reference.

To get behind this reference, the inventor went back to his notes. Now, if you recall, we mentioned that it is very important and a good thing for inventors to maintain diligent records of their inventions. Unfortunately, in this case, while the inventor did keep notes, his notes were terrible. The inventor tried to reconstruct the events to show due diligence and reduction to practice prior to the publication date of the Japanese reference, and in the course of doing so he made many mistakes.

As it turned out, the declarations were of no use in any event because the examiner held them to be insufficient, and he maintained the Japanese reference in the case and did not allow those claims that he felt were rendered obvious by that particular patent.

In court, the defendants argued that the mistakes in the declarations constituted willful misrepresentations to the Patent Office, constituting a third ground for inequitable conduct. The trial court agreed with them.

The issue for appeal on that finding once again goes to the question of intent. Intent cannot be inferred simply from the fact that there are inaccuracies in a document, and in this case the uncontroverted testimony by the inventor was that these mistakes were inadvertent. Also, the mistakes were given reasonable explanations in light of the way in which the notes were maintained. The court nonetheless concluded that the inaccuracies in the declarations were intentional. There was also an issue of materiality on that particular aspect of the case, since the patent examiner rejected the declarations in any event.

We have filed our briefs in that case and maybe by the time this book is published we will have an answer.

The case is of interest to me not simply because my client is involved and not simply because it involves some rather esoteric patent law considerations, but also because it goes to a very important evidentiary question that has implications far beyond the facts in this particular case. The evidentiary question is, precisely what may a court do in the face of uncontroverted testimony by witnesses that the court may disbelieve for reasons other than those present on the record? Since the order in this particular case was not prepared by the judge, there were no references to any subjective determinations, such as demeanor or tone of voice. Accordingly, there are a number of statements in the final judgment along the lines of "the court finds this witness's testimony to not be credible" without any explanation. It appears that this kind of thing does not happen all that often. In fact, we were not able to find a single case wherein a court stated that it disregarded uncontroverted testimony because of a witness's demeanor or any other subjective reason.

Incidentally, the judge who found inequitable conduct in this particular case was the same judge who overturned the record-setting judgment in *Litton v. Honeywell*, D.C.C. Cal. CV 90-93 MRP and CV 90-4823 MRP (1/6/95), on the basis of inequitable conduct of the lawyers who secured the patent on which *Litton* sued in that particular case. I mention this fact only because the *Litton* reversal was a very dramatic case involving the setting aside of a major jury verdict and also because these inequitable conduct defenses seldom succeed, and yet we have one judge who has found inequitable conduct on two cases in the same relative time frame.

Another note of interest in the *Litton* case is that the judge apparently did not reach the inequitable conduct issue until after the case had been tried. No doubt the judge felt that considerable time, effort, and angst would have been spared had there been a preliminary hearing on inequitable conduct, which would have eliminated the need for the rather extensive trial that followed and which ended up being of no import whatsoever (assuming the court is upheld on appeal).

In the *Tilton* case there also was an issue of inequitable conduct, because the defendants contended that Tilton had an obligation to inform the Patent Office about the testing of the clutch in races more than a year before the filing of the application. In that case, the issue of inequitable conduct was presented to the jury in a questionnaire, and the jury found no inequitable conduct. Thereafter, the trial judge adopted the finding of the jury. Rather than simply rubber-stamp the jury's finding, however, the judge wrote his own extensive and carefully reasoned opinion as to why there was no inequitable conduct.

I merely point this out so that you again have a flavor of the number of ways in which courts can handle these issues. In the *Litton* case, the court allowed the entire case to be tried before setting it aside on the basis of the court's independent finding of inequitable conduct. In my client's case, in front of the same judge, the court held the inequitable conduct hearing first (probably as a result of the experience in *Litton*), and in *Tilton* the court made its own determination of inequitable conduct after the case had been tried to a jury.

In *Tilton* it made sense to handle it the way it was handled, because the factual basis for the allegation of inequitable conduct (i.e., prior public use) contained essentially the same elements as the prior public use defense, which was a matter to be determined by the jury. It would have made little sense to spend an entire week trying the issue of inequitable conduct based on prior public use to the court and then retrying exactly the same issue to a jury. Not only would that have been impractical, but there might have been conflicting evidence and maybe even conflicting decisions.[1]

---

1. This raises another interesting issue, which we will save for a later day. In the meantime, however, we can be thinking about it. The questions are: If there is an equity issue to be made by the court and a legal determination to be made by a jury where the

underlying factual issue is identical, whose determination of the facts shall govern? May the court make its independent determination of the facts that is different from that of the jury? May the judge override the jury's determination on the facts? Is the court bound by the jury's determination on the facts?

I think I know the answer, but it doesn't fit into this particular discussion. Besides I want to leave you with something to think about.

20

Continuations, Divisions, and Continuations-in-Part

Continuations, divisions, and continuations-in-part all have to do with filing a patent and then continuing the prosecution process by either obtaining extensions of time for prosecution of the entire patent or parts of the patent, or by separating the patent into more than one patent because you have really tried to include two or more inventions in one.

A divisional application occurs when the patent examiner determines that the claims in the patent really are two separate inventions. This is nothing more than a ploy by the Patent Office to pick up some additional filing fees.[1] When that happens, the applicant has the option of electing one or the other set of claims and abandoning the rest, or filing a divisional application, which is nothing more than a separate application with the second set of claims.

A continuation application is an application filed while the first application is pending. The purpose in filing a continuation application is to add claims. Often continuation applications are filed for one or two strategic reasons. Because a continuation application is a separate patent application, it has a life of its own, independent of the original, filed

---

1. Incidentally, it is worth knowing, as part of your political education, that the Patent Office fees are used for more than simply sustaining office operations. There are periodic attempts to raise the fees and the patent bar usually vociferously objects. because higher fees are not necessary for the functioning of the patent office but are merely a ploy by the government to obtain additional funding for other purposes at the expense of people who have committed no crime other than to attempt to obtain a patent.

application. The only relationship between the two is that the specification must support the continuation application claims, and the continuation application has the benefit of the original filing date. Because the applications are treated as separate applications, the first application can issue as a patent while the continuation application remains pending. Also, an applicant can dismiss the original application and simply prosecute the continuation application. The question arises, what are the strategic reasons and advantages of having a continuation application pending?

Prior to the new patent statute, the life of a patent was measured from the date of issuance. Accordingly, a number of patent applicants used the continuation practice for what were known as submarine patents. That is, they would file a continuation application before the original patent issued and then dismiss the original application. In this manner, they were able to keep a patent application pending for a number of years. In the meantime, the technology would be advanced by others. The submarine applicant would then simply wait, and after the industry had developed and others had commercially developed the same technology, the submarine patentee would allow one of its continuation applications to ripen into a patent, and it would then sue the industry that had developed the technology independently during the time that the continuation applications were pending.

Under the new patent statutes, the lifetime of the patent exists from the date of the filing of the application. Accordingly, an individual who has a continuation application with a filing date going back 20 years would essentially have a meaningless patent issue, because it would have no remaining lifetime. As a result, the new patent statute will probably pretty much eliminate this submarine patent issue.

In *Symbol Techs. Inc. v. Lemelson Med.*, 277 F.3d 1361 (Fed. Cir. 2002), the court affirmed the defense of laches to a suit based on a continuation patent where intervening rights have been obtained by the accused infringer.

Besides the submarine issue, there is another reason for maintaining a continuation application. That reason is to maintain flexibility. If some third party were to come out with a device that would not read on the claims of the original application that issued as a patent, one would have the flexibility, with a continuation application, to either amend the claims in the continuation application or file a new continuation application with claims directed to a specific product. As a general rule, it is a good idea to always have a continuation application pending, at least while there is some meaningful lifetime remaining on any potential patent that might issue. Remember, however, that a continuation application can only be filed while there is an application pending. Once a patent has issued, one cannot file a continuation application.

A continuation-in-part is a continuation application that contains old matter (i.e., matter that is contained in the old application) and new matter. With regard to the new matter, the filing date is the date of the filing of the continuation-in-part. With regard to the old matter, of course, the filing date is that of the original application. In essence, a continuation-in-part is two separate patents in one.

21

How Continuation Practice (Like Everything Else) Can Be Confusing to a Judge

In a controversial decision, the Court of Appeals for the Federal Circuit in the case of *Gentry Gallery, Inc. v. Berkline Corp.,* 134 F.3d 1473 (Fed. Cir. 1998), held that a claim inserted by an amendment was invalid because it was lacking an essential element. In that case, the specification distinguished the patent over the prior art by location of the console used to operate a reclining sofa. In the original claims, that particular limitation was included. Before the patent issued, the patentee became aware of the fact that Berkline was making a sofa that had the console located in a different place. In order to have the patent reach the Berkline product, the claims were amended to remove the limitation of the location of the console.

The court, in invalidating the new claim, held that because of the statement in the specification differentiating the invention over the prior art by the location of the console, and also because of certain statements made by the inventor in his testimony in court, the particular location of the console was an essential element of the claims, and the claims that did not contain that limitation were invalid. What was particularly confusing about the court's decisions was the reference to the inventor's testimony. A more logical analysis would simply have been that the specification did not support the claims because the specification made it very clear that the location of the console was an essential part of the invention. Referencing the testimony of the inventor simply added confusion, and to date no reported cases have relied on the testimony of the inventor for determining that something was an essential element in a claim.

Subsequent to the issuance of the *Gentry Gallery* case, I represented Marty Reiffin in the case of *Reiffin v. Microsoft,* 214 F.3d 1342 (Fed. Cir. 2000). My representation was not in the original proceedings, but I wrote the brief for the appeal. (Reiffin, who is a patent lawyer in his own right, did his own oral argument before the CAFC and acquitted himself quite admirably.) The court below, in a bizarre decision that demonstrated a complete lack of understanding of the continuation process, invalidated Reiffin's patent on the basis of the *Gentry Gallery* decision.

The Reiffin patent involved what is commonly referred to as multi-threading. That is, it involved a program going back and forth between the writing of the program (or the using of the program) and a continuous checking of spelling, syntax, etc. That particular program is commonly used today, for example, in ongoing spell-checking, where an incorrectly spelled word is immediately underlined in red.

When Reiffin originally wrote his application, he was thinking in terms of writing programs. In the preferred embodiment, he used the example of a compiler. A compiler has at least two functions. The first function is to check for grammar, spelling, syntax, etc. The second function is to translate the source code into object code or machine-readable executable code. Reiffin's specification made it very clear that the invention concerned itself with the former aspect (i.e., syntax, spelling, etc.) and not with the translation function. Reiffin subsequently filed a continuation application and later abandoned the original application. In the continuation application, it specifically said that the use of the compiler was meant only as an example and that the invention could apply equally to any program involving the multithreading technique. That amendment was allowed by the Patent Office and was contained in the patent that eventually issued.

The original claims contained the compiler limitation. A number of the claims that finally issued contained no such limitation. The district court held that a compiler was an essential element of the claims (actually, I believe he called it an important element, thereby creating its own test) and cited *Gentry Gallery*. The problem was that the court did not understand continuation practice. In *Gentry Gallery*, the court looked to the specification of the patent that issued and determined that that specification required that the claims have the limitation of the location of the console. In *Reiffin*, the original application, which the lower court believed contained the limitation of a compiler, was abandoned. Accordingly, the patent specification, which involved the claims that the court invalidated, contained no such possible reservation or limitation. In addition, there was never a statement in any of the patents or patent applications that a compiler was an essential element or that the use of a compiler was a distinguishing feature over the prior art.

In doing a *Gentry Gallery*–type analysis, the court should have looked to the specification of the patent that finally issued, and not to the specification of a patent or patent application that was abandoned.

We were successful in the appeal. The court of appeals reversed and remanded to the court for further proceedings. The only real issue was whether the continuation contained new material that really would have made it a continuation-in-part and deprived Reiffin of the original filing date. Of course, the trial court never even undertook that analysis because of its fundamental misunderstanding of continuation practice. In point of actual fact, the removal of the compiler as a limitation did not constitute new matter. The use of a compiler was nothing more than an example of the manner in which the invention could be utilized. The same techniques described in the invention could and have been used in a number of different programs and is in wide use today.

22

How Do We Determine a Reasonable Royalty in Litigation?

One of the most perplexing and confusing areas of litigation involves the issue of how one determines a reasonable royalty in a patent infringement case. This dilemma stems from the fact that an infringer must pay damages that amount to no less than a reasonable royalty for infringement.

A common practice has been for patent lawyers to put on another patent lawyer who has experience in licensing to assert, basically out of thin air, what he believes would be a reasonable royalty. Often, people will put experts on to opine as to a reasonable royalty, with the plaintiff putting the royalty high and the defendant putting the royalty low. There are a number of cases detailing the arm's-length negotiating considerations that should be taken into account by juries and courts.

In my opinion, all of this is a lot of nonsense. It provides no evidence of the real world. The only useful evidence on reasonable royalties would be royalties actually paid in the industry for devices that are substantially similar. Bear in mind that royalties obtained in litigation or under threat of litigation are not admissible, and therefore those licenses are useless. The reality is that it is very difficult to find licenses on interchangeable items.

In my opinion (and I am going out on a limb here), reasonable royalties, from an economic analysis, are the same as lost profits. That is generally what you will hear from economists as opposed to accountants or patent lawyers. The theory is that a company that is in the business of making the patented product, and that has a patent on that product, will not give up any part of its profits to a competitor. The exception to that, of course, is if it would cost the patent owner extra money because it does not have the capacity to make the product. Most manufacturers do have the capacity to make the patented product, and therefore do not have any need whatsoever for a competitor to be out selling their product and taking a percentage of the profit. As a result, in the real world, no manufacturing patentee plaintiff would have any reason to accept anything less than the profit that the patentee-plaintiff could make from the sale of that product. In addition, there are other substantial advantages and benefits to selling the product. The most fundamental benefit is that it increases the customer base for the possible sale of other products as well as increasing the name recognition and reputation of the patent owner.

The question then is, why would the infringer be willing to pay the entire profit from the sale of the infringing product to the owner of the patent? The answer is, there is no incentive for a competitor to do so. Why would a competitor give up its entire profit? The answer relates again to the intangibles. Assuming the competitor has the capacity and does not have to expend additional funds, that competitor would obtain the advantage of an expanded customer base, expanded name recognition, enhanced reputation, and so on. Assuming the absence of additional investment risk, there would be no loss or downside to the infringer continuing to sell the infringing product at a break-even position. In fact, in the real world, business is rife with examples of companies operating at a loss, year after year, with the reasonable expectation that down the road their continued position in the marketplace will result in their making profits on other products. The automobile industry is a prime example.

The reasonable royalty issue, as discussed above, relates only to those cases in which the patentee-plaintiff is a manufacturer of the patented product. In other cases involving what I call the armchair inventor (i.e., one who is not in the business), it may be appropriate to have people opine as to what would be a reasonable royalty from the perspective of the infringer. In that case, there is an incentive for the armchair inventor to take less than his profit, because that inventor has no profit.

When I represent a patentee-manufacturer, I almost always ask for the lost profits and then tell the jury that they have the option of awarding a reasonable royalty, but if they decide to award a reasonable royalty, it should be no less than the lost profits for the reasons enunciated above.

In all candor, a number of people consider this a dangerous approach, but I believe it is the only one that makes sense. Allowing patent lawyers and others to opine out of the clear blue as to what would be a reasonable royalty creates a risk of losing credibility with the jury as well as giving the jury the option of awarding your client less than that to which he is entitled.

23

Forget Everything You Think You Know About the Statute of Limitations

If you went to law school, then you undoubtedly learned that the statute of limitations is a complete bar to the institution of a lawsuit. Because patent law, as well as patent lawyers, originated on another planet, patent law has a completely different meaning for the statute of limitations.

The statute of limitations in patent litigation does not serve as a complete bar to the institution of any litigation. It is rather a delineation of the time period over which one may collect damages. Under the patent statutes, one may only collect damages for six years' worth of infringement.

The one absolute defense in patent litigation is estoppel. Under estoppel, a defendant who effectively avails himself of this defense may preclude the litigation from proceeding against him at all. The requirements for estoppel are essentially the same as the requirements for laches in other types of cases—to wit, behavior by a plaintiff upon which a defendant reasonably and injuriously relies. There is no time period involved, although the courts will often use the six-year statute of limitations as a guideline.

It would be irresponsible and, in fact, reckless for a plaintiff to rely upon any particular time period. I had one case where my client was involved in patent infringement litigation against a first defendant. During the course of that litigation, the president of my client company came to me, while I was actually in court, and told me that he had accused another prospective defendant of infringement. He then informed me that the prospective defendant came to him and told him he was making a different product that he believed would not infringe. I asked my client what his position was with regard to the new product, and he said he believed it did infringe. I then told him that he'd better let the other fellow know that and/or he'd better get ready to sue him. Instead of doing so, my client simply let the matter lapse and decided to wait to see the outcome of the pending litigation. We were successful in the pending litigation, at which point my client instructed me to file suit against the other defendant.

The other defendant asserted a defense of estoppel, claiming that he had heard nothing further from my client and that he had gone ahead and begun manufacturing and selling the new product. The time period that had elapsed from the last conversation between my client and the defendant and the time of filing suit was only 18 months. Nonetheless, the court upheld the defense and threw our case out. The lesson in this is that your client should always follow your advice.

The other doctrine that is relevant in patent cases is laches. Again, this concept is different from the normal concept of laches that you were taught in law school. There you were taught that laches is essentially the statute of limitations, except that it involves estoppel considerations such as the ones related to the estoppel doctrine in patent law.

In patent law, however, laches does not bar the entire case. A successful assertion of laches in a patent case will prohibit an awarding of damages but will not prohibit the issuance of an injunction. In order to establish laches in a patent case, one must merely establish a failure to assert one's rights for a period of time beyond which one would expect someone to assert their rights. There is a presumption in laches that a delay of more than six years (the statute of limitations) before filing a lawsuit is an unreasonable length of time. Accordingly, failure to file a lawsuit for more than six years after the infringement begins may preclude one from recovering any damages whatsoever. It should be noted, however, that while the six-year laches period creates a presumption of laches, that presumption may be rebutted, depending upon circumstances. For example, licensing negotiations may toll the time period.

Laches is not available to a willing infringer. It should also be noted that while laches bars recovery of any damages prior to the filing of the lawsuit, that does not prohibit a patentee from obtaining damages subsequent to the filing of the lawsuit.

Interesting cases on the issue of laches include *A. C. Aukerman Company vs. R. L. Chadis Construction Company*, 960 F.2d 1020, 1028 (Fed. Cir. 1992); *Sun Studs, Inc. vs. A. T. A. Equipment Leasing, Inc.*, 17 U.S.P.Q. 2d, 1763, 1766 (D. Ore. 1990); and *Bourns, Inc. vs. Allen-Bradley Company*, 182 U.S.P.Q. 258, 259 (N.D. Ill.1974).

24

Patent Infringement, Tortious Interference, Unfair Competition, Declaratory Judgment—and Don't Forget Venue

As you may have surmised by now, these cases are very seldom limited to one or two issues. They often involve a number of related and interlocking issues that can arise in both the original complaint, the counterclaim, and sometimes even cross-complaints against third parties.

At this time I would like to discuss two cases in which I was involved that contained a number of overlapping and interrelating issues, including the all-important considerations of venue.

In *Automotive Products v. Tilton*, our client had invented a carbon-carbon clutch (this was discussed in a previous chapter). The lawyers in our office at Poms, Smith, Landy & Rose had written a number of letters to Automotive Products and to various customers of Automotive Products, including Porsche, who we believed were using our client's patented clutch in the United States. Automotive Products believed that our client's patent should never have issued and therefore could never be enforced. In support of its theory, it had gone to the Patent Office and sought reexamination of the claims of our client's patent in order to have them invalidated. The Patent Office rejected the reexamination petition, which should have been a fair warning to Automotive Products.

Instead of heeding that warning and letting sleeping dogs lie, Automotive Products decided to become aggressive. It filed an action for a declaratory judgment in Los Angeles seeking to have the patent declared invalid. This was a mistake for at least two reasons. First, in light of the rejection from the Patent Office on its request for reexamination, Automotive Products should have realized that its chances of having the patent declared invalid were extremely slim. Second, and far more important, our client had no intention of filing suit for patent infringement.

As a result of the filing of the declaratory judgment action, our client was left with no choice but to file a counterclaim for infringement. As part of our discovery, we requested all documents related to Tilton, including all documents relating to the termination of Tilton as a distributor of Automotive Products' products. The background on this was that Tilton was the exclusive distributor of Automotive Products' products in the United States. When Tilton accused Automotive Products of infringing its patent rights, and, more egregiously in Automotive Products' eyes, when Tilton began selling its clutch to Formula One race teams, which had always used Automotive Products' racing clutches in the past, Automotive Products decided to terminate Tilton as its distributor. It, of course, had every right to do so. We also knew, however, that Automotive Products had established a number of other distributors subsequent to its termination of Tilton. Accordingly, we requested all documents relating to these other distributorships.

As a result of our discovery, we obtained copies of the agreements between Automotive Products and its distributors as well as (after a considerable discovery battle) an internal memorandum outlining Automotive Products' approach to dealing with Tilton. In a memo titled "How to Deal with the Tilton Threat," it was stated that their policy would be to terminate Tilton as a distributor and thereafter establish a number of competing distributors in Tilton's geographical area to basically drive Tilton out of business. (Incidentally, that is my paraphrasing of the document; it is not meant to be taken as a literal statement of what was contained therein. This particular document was introduced in evidence and is probably available as part of the court's records to anybody who wishes to review it.) We also obtained copies of all the distributor agreements, all of which contained a clause prohibiting them from doing any business with Tilton.

As a result of obtaining all of this additional information, we amended our counterclaim for patent infringement to include tortious interference, violation of the U.S. antitrust laws, and unfair competition under California law.

We ended up being awarded a relatively small amount for patent infringement because all the sales took place in England, even though the products were later shipped to the United States. It should be noted that under the new patent laws, those sales would have been considered infringing sales, whether or not the actual invoices were paid in a foreign country. Nonetheless, that was the law at that time, so our patent infringement losses were relatively small. The jury awarded a substantial sum for violation of the antitrust laws as well as an additional sum for tortious interference. Because the antitrust laws are trebled and the court had the discretion to treble the patent infringement damages, and because the court had an obligation to award attorney's fees for the antitrust portion of the case as well as the discretion to award attorney's fees for the patent part of the case, Tilton obtained a judgment that included trebling of all damages as well as the awarding of all fees and costs.

As far as the unfair competition was concerned, the court threw out that portion of the case because it said the unfair competition actions occurred in England, not in the state of California, and therefore were not actionable in California.

This case, which started out as a simple declaratory judgment action and ended up resulting in a substantial judgment for a number of causes of action, would never have been filed had the defendant not initiated the litigation in the first place. It is a prime example of why it is so important for corporate counsel and litigation counsel to review all of their clients' records and spot any potential areas for counterclaims before embarking upon litigation. It is always important to not only consider what you would like to do, but consider what the other side may want to do as well.

In another case, we filed a complaint for patent infringement on behalf of our client. We filed the case in the Eastern District of Virginia, which is commonly called the "rocket docket" because the cases get to trial in a matter of months, which, for a plaintiff, is often a distinct advantage.

The defendant immediately attempted to move the venue of the case from the Eastern District of Virginia to Southern California. Since my office is in Southern California, you might assume that I would have been delighted with the attempt to change venue and would not have opposed the motion. Of course, the defendant's reason for attempting to move the case was so that they could delay it, which was exactly the reason we had not filed it in Southern California in the first place. (For the record, Southern California is the least favorable place to file any lawsuit because it is the most understaffed and inefficient district in the country, and it is virtually impossible to get a civil case to trial.)

We had originally filed a case against both the U.S. company and its German parent. In support of its motion, the defendant filed affidavits asserting that the U.S. company had substantial independence from the German parent company and went through a list of factors showing how independent the two companies were. The motion was denied in short order. (Another advantage of the Eastern District of Virginia is that motions are usually decided within a week, which is how it ought to be; there is no excuse for these other courts taking as long as they do to decide simple motions.)

In the course of discovery, we unearthed documents that led us to believe there was arguably a conspiracy between the German company and the U.S. company regarding pricing of products as it related to the plaintiff. Since the U.S. company was a partially owned subsidiary of the German company, one has to ask, how can there be a conspiracy? It is well-established law that a corporation cannot conspire with itself. This includes the ability of a corporation to conspire with its wholly owned subsidiaries. What does this mean with regard to partially owned subsidiaries? Well, the answer is that there is a division of authority. In reviewing the positions of various courts across the country, we discovered that in the Third Circuit, a corporation may conspire with a partially owned subsidiary provided certain criteria of independence are established. It just so happened that almost all of those criteria were set forth by the U.S. defendant in support of its motion for change of venue from the Eastern District of Virginia to California. Accordingly, we felt very comfortable in filing an antitrust suit for conspiracy in the Third Circuit. Since the U.S. company imported into New Jersey (which is in the Third Circuit), we filed a separate cause of action in New Jersey alleging violation of the antitrust laws.

Whether our theory was valid or not we'll never know, because, unfortunately, that case settled.[1] Regardless of the fact that the case settled, we clearly were provided with the opportunity to bring an antitrust action based upon pleadings that had been filed by the U.S. company in support of a different objective. That is why every action taken in these cases must be seriously reviewed in terms of its violation of the law of unintended consequences. Cases are often like complicated chess matches: One has to be aware not only of one's own moves, but also of the potential moves of the other party.

The above case illustrates some of the considerations relating to venue. An overarching venue consideration should be made before filing any patent infringement or antitrust case. Usually, in patent cases, a wide variety of venues is available because the parties usually do business nationwide. Contrary to the prevailing wisdom that the best thing to do for a client is to file the suit in the geographical location that is most convenient, I believe the analysis should be made in terms of likelihood of moving the case through the court system as rapidly as possible.

---

1. I hate to settle cases. This is why I always try to avoid reasonable clients. Reasonable clients should not hire Irish lawyers.

For example, I recently filed a copyright infringement case in Texas. Both parties reside primarily in California, but both of them do business in Texas. In my opinion, the federal courts in Texas are not only among the fastest in the country, they are also among the best. Courts in all of the districts of Texas usually provide good decisions, and they provide them rapidly. I frankly wish that our California federal judges would be required to attend a seminar taught by the judges in Texas and Virginia every six months. If, perhaps, they did, our cases might move at something faster than a snail climbing a glacier.

25

What Have You Learned?

Now that we have run all around the mulberry bush, let's go back and pick up the loose ends and see if we can figure out what you've learned, if anything, from what you've read so far.

1. *What part of a patent do you look at to determine whether there is infringement?*

    The answer is "The claims! The claims!" (No, not "The plane! The plane!" That's from another show.)

2. *Who founded the U.S. Patent Office?*

    This is a trick question. If you know the answer, you didn't get it from this book because I never mentioned it. The answer is Thomas Jefferson.

3. *Why did Thomas Jefferson create the U.S. Patent Office?*

    He had nothing better to do on that particular day, and he wanted an excuse to get out of the house. Also, he was always inventing things and never getting paid for them. The Patent Office was just another failed money-making scheme like the University of Virginia. He died broke and in debt like all great men such as Mozart and probably me.

4. *Why bother getting a patent?*

    The answer is so that you can keep your job. The other answer is so you can have something neat to put on your wall and something to brag about to your friends. An alternate answer is so you can protect your technology and have the exclusive right to make, use, and sell that technology for a limited period of time.

5. *What is the lifetime of a patent?*
    Twenty years from the date of the filing of the application for a utility patent and 14 years from the date of issue for a design patent.

6. *What is the best way for a lawyer to think of a patent?*
    A lawyer should *always* think of a patent as a trial exhibit.

7. *How should a lawyer think of all documents relating to obtaining a patent, including lawyer's notes and files as well as inventor's records, in-house memoranda, correspondence, etc.?*
    They all should be thought of as potential trial exhibits and treated accordingly at all times.

8. *What are the bars to obtaining a patent?*
    *   Trying to patent something previously invented by someone else in any country: 35 U.S.C. 102(f).
    *   Trying to patent something patented or published in any country more than a year before your filing date: 35 U.S.C. 102(b).
    *   Trying to patent something in prior public use *in the U.S.A.* more than a year before your filing date: 35 U.S.C. 102(a).
    *   (Check out 35 U.S.C. 102 (a)–(g) for a complete list.)

9. *What is patent prosecution?*
    The process of shepherding a patent application through the Patent Office until it becomes an actual patent.

10. *What is file wrapper estoppel?*
    Being held to what your no-good lawyer said during patent prosecution when he was desperately trying to save his own skin and sell you down the river by saying anything to get your stupid patent. It usually means you can't get broader claims when you specifically narrowed them to convince the examiner to allow your patent to issue, thus resulting in your having a patent that isn't worth the cost of the match to burn it.

11. *Who may obtain a patent?*
    Anyone who has
    (a) actually invented something;

      (b) not publicly used or disclosed the invention in the United States for more than a year before filing of the application in the United States (or in many other countries not having publicly used or disclosed it at all); and

      (c) the big bucks to shell out to a patent lawyer and the patience to wait while the patent lawyer and the patent examiner exchange esoteric bons mots.

12. *What is public use or sale?*

    Who knows? Some things are obvious, such as if you go around selling your product to anyone who will buy it. Others are not quite so obvious, such as making a sidewalk out of wooden planks and having people walk over it for 10 years to see if it will last that long. These have to be decided on a case-by-case basis, but you should at least understand the principles.

13. *What is anticipation?*

    Anticipation means looking forward to finishing this book. It also means looking forward to winning the lottery or that Ed McMahon thing, where they come around and televise you making a fool out of yourself for a lousy few million bucks. In patent law, it means that prior art that is identical in claim language to what has either been invented or is seeking to be patented. If the anticipatory reference has been in existence before the actual invention by the patentee or prospective patentee, it invalidates the patent or prevents it from issuing in the first place. The same is also true if the anticipatory reference was published either in the United States or abroad more than a year before the filing date or if it was in public use in the United States more than a year before the filing date.

14. *What is obviousness?*

    Obviousness is a lot like anticipation, except that it really means combining two or more references to come up with the invention, and it would be obvious to one skilled in the art to do so.

15. *What is infringement?*

    An infringing product is one that reads on the claims of a patent. Actually, it may be the other way around—that is, the claims of the patent may read on the infringing product; I never have been able to figure out which is which. In any event, it means you take the product and you match that product to each and every one of the elements of the claim, and if they are all there, then you have an infringing product. That, of course, is "literal infringement."

There is also infringement by the doctrine of equivalents, which means even though there may be some variations in the accused product from the literal terminology of a term in a claim, the accused product nonetheless performs essentially the same function in essentially the same manner to achieve essentially the same result as that particular claim element.

It is an equitable doctrine intended to prevent a person from utilizing all of the principles of the invention and yet seeking to avoid infringement by making meaningless variations from the literal terminology in the claims. The determination of whether a product infringes either literally or under the doctrine of equivalents is a matter for the jury to decide (i.e., the finder of fact), unless a court decides it on summary judgment after an analysis of the claim elements and their comparison to the accused product or process.

In addition to direct infringement, which means the making or selling of a product that infringes, there is also contributory infringement and inducement of infringement. Contributory infringement means selling a part that is not a staple article of commerce that is then used in an infringing product. Inducement of infringement means just what it says: You induce someone to infringe someone else's patent. Both contributory and inducement of infringement require intent.

16. *What is the difference between a U.S. patent and a foreign patent?*
This is pretty simple. A U.S. patent is one that issues in the United States, and a foreign patent is one that issues in a foreign country. Actually, this whole subject matter is one that should be included in treaties on international relations. There are, in fact, a number of treaties relating to filings in one country and the effect of those filings in other countries. For example, under the Patent Cooperation Treaty (PCT), you can file an application in the United States and use that filing date as the filing date in foreign countries. This becomes particularly important when dealing with countries wherein a patent is barred if it is in prior public use or sale for even one day before the filing of the patent application.

Under the PCT, a person can file in the United States and at the same time file a PCT form, and thereafter publicly use the invention without having waived his or her foreign patent rights. There are complications, however, in filing a foreign patent, particularly in the area of disclosure. In many, if not most, foreign countries, a patent application is published before the patent actually issues. This is completely contrary to the policy in the United States, wherein patent applications are maintained in secret until such time as they actually issue. The publication of a European patent application may serve as prior art and may act as a bar to the filing of subsequent applications either in the United States or abroad, depending on when such additional patent applications are filed. This subject goes on and on and becomes more and more complicated; therefore, I am going to stop while you are ahead.

17. *What is the first-to-file rule?*

The first-to-file rule (which is the rule in virtually every country but the United States) says that the first person to file for an application is the one who gets the patent, regardless of who was the first to invent. In the United States we are virtually alone in having the first-to-invent rule, which means that regardless of who files first, it is the first to invent who is entitled to the patent. In the United States, when two patents are co-pending by different inventors, they go into what is known as an "interference" proceeding in the U.S. Patent Office. While the U.S. rule is by far the more fair and equitable rule, the first-to-file rule is much easier to administer and enforce, and most people suspect that the United States will soon move to a first-to-file system.

18. *What is discovery?*

Discovery is what someone does when they invent something, as in, "Eureka, I have discovered a new invention." Actually, that is a misuse of the term "discovery." A patent issues to a person who invents something, not one who discovers something. A person who merely discovers something, such as a mathematical formula or a substance existing in nature, is not entitled to a patent. Discovery is also a term that relates to litigation, and if you do not know what it means by now, then you're obviously not a lawyer.

19. *Can you litigate a patent infringement case in a state court?*

The answer is both yes and no. Let's deal with no first. If you sue someone for patent infringement, that must be tried in a federal court because under the Constitution the laws governing inventions are federal, so state law is preempted and the federal claims must be determined by the federal courts. Nonetheless, patent issues are sometimes litigated in state courts. For example, if you are litigating a contract issue over who has the rights to a patent, this can be litigated in state court even though it might involve a number of patent issues. Another area where patents are sometimes litigated in state court is trade secrets.

I tried a case once in state court where my client was accused of stealing another person's trade secrets relating to processes concerning rare earth oxides. Our defense in that case was that the technology that my client was accused of stealing was already well known in the art, and we based this defense on disclosures in approximately 50 different patents.

Other cases involving patents in state court may relate to who has the rights to a patent based on employment or access to information, who has the right under an employment contract to use information obtained during the course of that employment, and so on.

20. *Who owns the rights to a patent?*

The inventor, or if the inventor is employed and the invention is developed during the course and scope of his or her employment on the job using the employer's facilities, the employer has the rights to the invention. This also can be the subject of a specific contract provision between the inventor and others.

21. *Is that all there is to know about patents?*

Yes. Everything that anyone needs to know about patents has been set forth in this section.

Section 3

Trademarks

26

Trademarks, Service Marks, and Unfair Competition

The most common misconception about trademarks et al. is that they exist for the benefit of the trademark owner. They do not. They exist for the benefit of the consumer.

Another important point to remember is that while patents and copyrights have a limited duration, trademarks are forever. (I know what you're thinking—this sounds like a great title for a movie.)

Even though trademarks exist forever, they also can be lost at a moment's notice. How do we reconcile these two concepts? That is one of those interesting questions that relates to the esoterica of abstract issues and parallel universes. Since we don't have time for that kind of a discussion, however, we will try to keep this on a mundane plane.

The key is what I mentioned above, which is that a trademark is for the benefit of the consumer. Its purpose is to identify the origin of a particular product, so that if I buy a product with the Xerox name on it, I know I am buying a product manufactured by Xerox. This is why when trademarks are assigned or sold, they are not simply assigned or sold in blank. Always accompanying these agreements is the transfer of the "goodwill" associated with the mark. This is because it is the goodwill of the company and its recognition that is the real value in the trademark.

A common misconception is that the best trademark is the one that is most descriptive. In fact, that is not only *not* the best trademark, it is the worst. One of the main grounds for denying trademark registration is that the mark is merely descriptive. Another and related ground is that the mark is generic. In other words, a mark that identifies a product by its generic or its descriptive name may accurately identify the product but does nothing to identify the manufacturer or seller.

Not surprisingly, the best trademark is one that bears no reasonable relationship to anything. One of the best examples around is Xerox. At first glance, one might try to pronounce it "X-rox," but of course this sounds far too much like Ex-Lax, which has contributed to far too many bad-taste jokes, and so we say "Zerox." I guess it's all a matter of whose ox is being gored.

The theory is that you create the value of your own mark. You do this by advertising, marketing, selling a good product, etc. It's amazing how many people come to my office with what they consider to be a dynamite trademark because it really sets out in the public's mind the nature of the product or service. What these people believe is that the mark will provide the market. They have it exactly in reverse: It is the marketing that gives value to the mark. What is surprising is not that so many people have that misconception, because it is perfectly natural, but how many of them refuse to believe me when I tell them to get rid of the descriptive or generic mark because it probably won't be able to be registered anyway, and even if it is, it probably would be knocked out somewhere down the line. Some of these people remind me of that old Monty Python skit where the guy pays for an argument and he goes in and says, "I am here for my argument," and the staff person says, "No you aren't," and it goes on from there.

Just so the record is clear, the mere fact that there is some description in a mark does not in and of itself mean that the mark is automatically invalid or can't serve as a trademark. What the mark cannot be is "merely descriptive" or generic. Some degree of description is allowable. The problem is that this always becomes a matter of judgment. My advice to the client is usually, "Don't spend a lot of money and time and effort trying to convince an examiner to allow a mark that contains some description if you have not already put money into that mark."

Even though a trademark is forever, you can lose it at any time. The reason a mark is forever is that once a product has been identified with a certain mark in the mind of the public, the public has a right to rely on that mark as long as that company is making the product. On the other hand, if the product name becomes so familiar to the public that it becomes generic, then you lose the mark. A prime example of this is the Monopoly game. Because Parker Bros. did not carefully safeguard its trademark on the name "Monopoly," it lost it. The game of Monopoly, according to the judge who tried that case, is now a generic term, and so when people hear the term "Monopoly," they think of a particular type of game, as opposed to a particular company that makes it.

Examples of marks that are carefully guarded are Xerox and Kleenex. Even though people commonly refer to copying as xeroxing, you will never hear a lawyer for Xerox making such a remark. The correct term is photocopying on a Xerox brand copier. By the same token, you will never see an ad for Kleenex. Those marks are very carefully designated as "Kleenex brand facial tissues."

How do you go about getting a trademark? In many Latin American countries, all you have to do is file a trademark. A number of our clients have found, to their chagrin, when they went to do business south of the border, that their well-established trademarks in the United States had been claimed by local residents as their own. They have had to purchase the trademark rights to their own products. Accordingly, we always advise our clients that if they are going to be expanding to foreign markets, they should register their trademarks in those countries before someone else does.

In this country we have a slightly different criterion. To register a trademark, you first have to have used it in interstate commerce. You also can register trademarks under various state laws, and in those situations, the mark only has to have been used in the state where it is seeking to be registered.

Under recent procedures, one can also reserve a trademark in the Patent and Trademark Office for a limited period of time, but it still must be used before it is registered.

27

Trademarks— Use Them or Lose Them

When we were talking about obtaining a trademark (or service mark), we said that the key is to use it and, if it is a federally registered mark, to use it in interstate trade or commerce. Using a mark in interstate trade or commerce could be as simple as selling a product in a different state from the one in which it is manufactured or, in the case of a service mark, advertising it in a publication that is circulated in more than one state. For a trademark to be registered, it must not be generic or merely descriptive. It can be somewhat descriptive or arbitrary or fanciful. (Again, arbitrary or fanciful is preferred.) In addition, no one can have registered the mark before you. That is fairly common sense and obvious, but questions arise when someone else has a trademark either similar to the one you want to use or identical to the one you want to use but that has been put on products that are somewhat different from your products.

Remember, a trademark is a mark that is actually affixed to a product being sold. To obtain a registration of that trademark, you must fill in a form (don't you always?) and attach copies of the labels, boxes, or other item to which the trademark is actually affixed. A service mark, on the other hand, is a mark used in connection with a service, such as a restaurant, dry cleaners, exterminators, etc.

There are two registers, the Principal Register and the Supplemental Register, for trademark registrations. The Principal Register is for actual marks to which trademark registration has been granted. The Supplemental Register is where marks that are questionable can be placed for a limited period of time. If after a time (usually five years) the applicant can demonstrate that the marks have become associated in the mind of the public with the particular manufacturer or service provider, then those marks may be transferred to the Principal Register. Being on the Supplemental Register also allows the use of the mark ® and the right to sue in federal court.

Trademark registrations are divided into various classes or groupings of products or services. Different persons may use the same trademark if the trademark use is for such distinctively different products or services that there is not any real danger of confusion in the minds of the public.

Since the federal trademark registration is national, persons who have registered their federal trademarks may arguably claim that they have exclusive rights throughout the country. There are exceptions to this, however. If your mark has been used primarily in a given geographical area, then others may have rights to the same mark in different geographical areas if theirs have been limited as well. This is often true in the case of restaurants, where one may find the same name attributed to different restaurants that are not chains but simply local restaurants that may advertise in papers of interstate circulation, but where there is really no danger of confusing a restaurant in California named George's Black-Eyed Bistro (I made that up) with a restaurant by the same name in the Ozarks.

Because trademarks are, as we indicated previously, for the benefit of the public, the Trademark Office does not limit itself merely to a search of registered trademarks to see if there has been prior potentially confusing use of the mark submitted for registration, it looks to nonregistered uses of the mark as well. It is for this reason that one considering the potential registration of a mark (or even the use of a mark) should conduct a thorough search not only of the Patent and Trademark Office registered marks but also in yellow pages, corporate registers, etc. There are companies such as Thomson & Thomson that will perform services of varying scope for varying prices. These searches do not take very long and are well worth the money.

So, you filed your trademark or service mark application, and after some back and forth with the trademark examiner, who has pulled marks similar to yours but not identical and on slightly different products, and who has also argued that your mark is too descriptive, you have finally worn him down and convinced him to allow the registration of your mark. Congratulations! You're finished, right? Wrong. The mark will be published for a limited period of time, and the public will have the opportunity to come in and challenge your right to the mark. There are companies that have whole teams of people who constantly are searching the Federal Register to see if anybody is attempting to register a name that they don't like. If this happens and a mark is challenged, it will be resolved by the Patent and Trademark Office in a manner satisfactory to all sides. (Right!)

OK, you've finally done it. Your client's trademark has been registered and now you can forget about it, right? Wrong. The first complication is that between the fifth and sixth years of registration you have to file a declaration or affidavit of continued use. If you don't file those declarations, you will lose your registration. Accordingly, most people who have registered trademarks and who also have lawyers who know what they are doing calendar the declaration filing dates. There is a reason for this procedure, other than to keep certain people employed and to provide a nuisance and annoyance to others. (Although that is obviously the prime reason.) The reason is the rationale for trademarks in the first place. If you have used a mark for a short period of time and then abandoned it, you can expect that the public will stop associating that mark with your client's product or services. Accordingly, someone else should have a shot.

The next problem that comes up is from that perpetual source of aggravation, your client's competitors. There is nothing more annoying to a business than a competitor, but unfortunately there is no way to eliminate them other than by engaging in illegal antitrust activities (a subject for another book) or by engaging in socially unacceptable activities such as homicide, mayhem, aggravated assault, destruction of property, libel and slander, or unfair competition.

During the first five years of registration, a trademark has a presumption of validity. However, if competitors use your client's mark and you sue them, they can challenge your mark as being descriptive or they can claim that they had prior use themselves or use any one of a myriad of trademark defenses aimed at invalidating your client's trademark.

After the first five years and the filing of your declaration, your client's trademark is generally incontestable, except for a number of notable exceptions, primarily the "gang of eight," which are:

(1) Fraud in obtaining the registration or the status of incontestability;
(2) Abandonment;
(3) Use of the mark to misrepresent source;
(4) "Fair use" of the mark;
(5) Limited territory defense of an intermediate junior user;
(6) Prior registration of defendant;

(7) Use of the mark to violate federal antitrust law; and

(8) Equitable defenses such as laches, estoppel, and acquiescence.

If your client's trademark is incontestable, the only question then becomes whether someone's use of the alleged infringing mark is identical to your client's and used on the same subject matter (a no-brainer), is so similar to your client's mark as to create confusion, or is used on products sufficiently similar to your client's products to cause confusion.

28

Trademark Infringement

The subject of trademark infringement, as is the case with so many intellectual property matters, sounds very simple on its face, but it often becomes complicated in the application. The general theory of trademark infringement again goes to the philosophical basis for trademarks, which is that their purpose is to prevent consumer confusion. Accordingly, the objective test to determine if there is trademark infringement is whether there is a false designation of origin of the products that causes consumers to buy a product from one company, believing that those products were manufactured by another company.

As a first preliminary step, bear in mind that there are different types of trademarks. There is the most common form of trademark, the federally registered trademark, which is the mark that one most usually thinks of as a trademark. Most of the well-known products with which we are familiar have federally registered trademarks. There are also state-registered trademarks, and there are common-law trademarks. A common-law trademark is a mark that is used but not necessarily registered.

There are also different laws under which trademark rights may be asserted. In addition to the Lanham Act, which provides for suit on federally registered trademarks and false designation of origin, there is also common-law unfair competition, which has been generally described as palming off, or false designation of origin, which may or may not be coextensive with infringement of a registered trademark.[1]

The classic case of trademark competition is where someone in some unscrupulous foreign country is making a bunch of counterfeit U.S. products and slapping a counterfeit label on them. The unscrupulous cads and bounders who engage in this activity try to smuggle them into the United States, and they are either stopped at the border by an order from the International Trade Commission directing the seizure by customs agents or they get into this country and are seized in the back of a flatbed truck pursuant to a midnight search-and-seizure order.

Those cases are no-brainers, and the scoundrels are usually locked up after all of their material has been confiscated and destroyed. This particular issue has recently gained some high-level attention because of our trade talks with China.

A tougher issue is what happens when legitimate businesses are using marks that may or may not be confusingly similar, depending on the facts of the case and who is making the determination. Now, as a diligent and well-educated lawyer versed in our legal system, you would probably say, "Hey, if it's not a dead-bang right-on no-brainer, it's obviously a matter for the trier of fact, a jury." Well, that's what I usually think too, but when I think that, I'm wrong.

For example, I had a case back in the distant recesses of the early 1980s involving a restaurant in New Hampshire that had a registered service mark that I will call (I am making this up) The Robin Hood Bar & Grill. Another restaurant, also in New Hampshire but in a different city, was called the The Robin Hood Cafe. We sued, armed not only with the registered service mark but also with declarations from a number of people who testified that they thought the restaurants were somehow related. We appeared before a judge who was unintelligible. (I was later informed that this was the result of his having a speech impediment called the New Hampshire accent.) As soon as I heard him speaking in New Hampshire, I realized immediately why I'll never run for president. Not only is the primary weather in New Hampshire dev-

---

1. Unfair competition can also mean competing unfairly, which is an extremely broad characterization. What actually constitutes unfair competition and what are the appropriate remedies for various types of unfair competition are extremely complicated subjects of their own, particularly as they get into the whole issue of insurance coverage and duties to defend where unfair competition is considered as part and parcel of advertising injury. This is a subject for a whole separate volume in an extremely important and newly evolving area of the law. Fortunately, we are not going to be discussing that now, because this is a section on trademarks, not insurance coverage, unfair competition, and all that other stuff.

astating, but no one who is from there can understand what anybody who is not from there is saying. Since most politicians are unintelligible in any event, the result is complete political anarchy, which goes a long way toward explaining why we have the leadership we have. But enough about my opinions.

After a full day of wrangling, the judge finally looked down and said, "I'll take it under advisement." That, of course, is judicial code for "I am going to rule against you, but I don't have any good reasons, so I don't want you here when I tell you." I don't know which is worse, judges who rule against you behind your back or ones that tell you to your face that they don't care what you have to say, they simply are not going to listen. I suppose when you have a job for life, you don't worry about offending anyone.

Not surprisingly, he ruled against us. I say "not surprisingly" not because of the merits but because of his attitude. He simply made the pronouncement that in his opinion the marks were not confusingly similar and not likely to create confusion. While we could have appealed his order, it is highly unlikely we would have been successful, since he correctly spelled out the criteria and gave his judicial, totally subjective, opinion.

In another case in the Northern District of California, I had a client that was purchasing and thereafter modifying certain Hewlett-Packard products. It then repackaged those products in the original Hewlett-Packard box and inserted that box into a larger box of its own that had a plastic window through which one could see the original Hewlett-Packard box along with various replacement parts provided by my client. The second box into which the original Hewlett-Packard box was placed contained markings on it indicating that the product being sold was a modified Hewlett-Packard product; it spelled out in some detail the manner in which the products were modified; it had my client's name prominently displayed on the box; and it contained a statement that my client was not affiliated with Hewlett-Packard in any way.

Nonetheless, in spite of all of these markings, the court in an ex parte TRO proceeding accepted Hewlett-Packard's position as to trademark infringement and likelihood of confusion (even though Hewlett-Packard had not one declaration from any consumer who had ever been confused) and issued a temporary restraining order. There was the required hearing after seizure, and the court refused to reconsider its opinion and affirmed that there was indeed likelihood of confusion in maintaining the seizure order. Subsequently the case was transferred to another judge, who merely rubber-stamped the opinion of the first judge and then granted summary judgment against my client, stating the conclusion that there was likelihood of confusion and therefore trademark infringement. There was never any attempt by the court to hear conflicting testimony as to the likelihood of confusion, and since there was no evidence of actual confusion, the court's decision was made entirely on the subjective evaluation of the original judge who entered the original ex parte TRO, without any real independent analysis by the second judge.

Trademark Infringement Damages

There are two ways of calculating damages in a trademark case. In the first place, there must be some actual damages. One way to show damages is to show that the damaged party actually suffered lost sales or dilution of its trademark. This is a tough one, and if a business actually can show that its trademark was infringed by a competitor, which resulted in proven damages, it probably will have other causes of action, including tortious interference with a prospective business advantage (which carries punitive damages) and lots of others, which will be discussed in another book.

Sometimes damages can be inferred from the profits made by another. In other words, it may be possible to convince the trier of fact that another person's sales would have been your client's sales. Now, obviously, you are not entitled to gross sales. The question then becomes, "How do you calculate profits?" The obvious approach is to look at the profits the other guy made and say, "Well, his profits would have been our profits." Now all we have to do is show his gross sales, then let him show the offset, and then we are entitled to the balance; and if he can't show his costs, then we are entitled to his gross sales.

This, of course, is not an intellectually pure analysis. To be totally pure, one should point to the other fellow's gross sales and then show what your costs would have been, thereby showing what your profit would have been if his sales had been yours.

Unlike copyright and patent damages, there is no provision for reasonable royalties, since we are not talking about protecting the rights to a creative enterprise. Of course, if you are involved in a situation where there are counterfeit products being brought in from a foreign country and sold in bulk, then damages relating to the other fellow's sales may be well worth the trouble.

Usually, where a major enterprise is protecting its trademarks, the injunction issue is pretty quick; therefore, damages are not usually a major issue in these kinds of cases. When the damages per se are not a big issue, the focus tends to switch toward costs and attorney's fees. This is because there is a provision in the trademark laws that attorney's fees may be awarded *at the discretion* of the court. These fees usually should be awarded in a situation where there is actual counterfeiting, and even then the court does not have to award all of the attorney's fees. The court may award them in whole or in part.

29

Trade Dress Infringement

We have alluded briefly to trade dress infringement above, but it is not a bad idea to have it broken out separately because it does have some interesting aspects and considerations of its own.

As you all know by now, you can register a trademark on just about anything. Incidentally, there are all kinds of things that can qualify as trademarks, including colors, logos, words, phrases, even a person's name or the name of a state or a city. Harley-Davidson is trying to trademark a sound. It is ironic that sometimes people are prohibited from using even their own names in conjunction with their business because someone else has trademarked their name.

In addition to a registered mark, a product also may have a significant trade dress with which the public identifies the source of origin of that product. A prime example is the Louis Vuitton purses. In other words, if someone were selling purses (as one defendant obviously did) that had the same marking as the Louis Vuitton purse, that would be a violation of Louis Vuitton's trade dress rights, because people buying those purses would think they were buying purses made by Louis Vuitton, with all of the quality that the name implies.

One principle to bear in mind at all times in trade dress cases is that the trade dress in question *must be ornamental and not functional.* If there is a particular design that of necessity grows out of the function of the device, then there is no protection.

I had a case once in the Central District of California (*Quantum v. Soong*) involving automatic satellite positioning devices for use with TV satellite dishes. There were many counts in the case, but one of them was for trade dress infringement. The plaintiff in that case (I represented the defendant, thank the Lord) alleged, among other things, that he had designed these control boxes in a distinct fashion so that anyone looking at them would immediately associate them with him. Of course, one of the plaintiff's problems was that the boxes were not designed by him at all, but were, in fact, designed by a company in Taiwan that had been retained by my client to design and make these boxes. Nonetheless, the trade dress issue in that case had to do with (1) whether the design of the boxes was distinctive and ornamental versus functional, and (2) whether there was any reason to believe that they were associated in the public mind with that particular plaintiff. (To end the suspense, there was no such evidence presented at court.)

With regard to the design itself, the plaintiff, on cross-examination, was very proud of the fact that everything shown on the face of the control box was absolutely necessary to its functioning. The device itself was essentially a rectangular box with the necessary dials and a run-of-the-mill numerical LED display. As a result, there was a finding that there was no distinctive trade dress and, frankly, my feeling at the time was, and still is, that that issue should not even have gone to the jury.

I do know of other cases, however, involving essentially the same issue, i.e., that all of the elements as shown on the outside of the device were necessary to its use, and yet these cases were presented to juries who determined that there was, in fact, fanciful trade dress. Since one can arrange bells and whistles and nuts and bolts and dials in any number of fashions, it is theoretically possible to argue that the choice of arrangement has some particular distinctive aesthetic appearance, and if enough customers can be found to testify that they associate that particular arrangement of features with a particular manufacturer to the exclusion of others, there is always the potential of winning one of these cases on a theory of trade dress.

30

Unfair Competition

What is unfair competition? This is one of the thorniest, most complicated, and least well-defined issues in the law. In California there is statutory unfair competition, which is defined in the broadest possible terms.
A cause of action brought under the California Business and Professions
Code §§ 17200 et seq. is not triable to a jury but is a matter of equity for
the court.

In a recent case, the plaintiff (which I represented) filed the complaint (before I got involved in the case) alleging trade secret theft and
unfair competition. The trade secret theft cause of action was triable to a
jury, while the unfair competition cause of action was to be decided by
the court. The jury was unable to decide the trade secret issue and split
right down the middle, resulting in a hung jury.

Thereafter, the court decided that since it was the court's responsibility to determine the inequitable conduct issue, the court had a right to
decide all of the issues in the case, since the facts were overlapping. The
court then decided the unfair competition issue against my client, and,
having done so, proceeded to decide the trade secret theft issue against
my client as well. The court, of course, then denied the request to have
the case retried. The law is abundantly clear in every jurisdiction that a
person has a right to trial by jury of those issues that are triable to a jury,
and the fact that there is a concurrent parallel cause of action triable by
the court does not in any jurisdiction, including California, result in the
denial of the right to trial by jury. In fact, we cited to the court a Califor-

nia Supreme Court case that reversed a court for doing precisely what the court did in this instance. The court in this case indicated that while there might be a split of authority, there was still a legal basis for its decision. In support of its decision, the court relied on some real estate cases wherein the equitable issue of title was determined before the legal issues of right of possession.

This case was shocking, not only because of the clear error made by the court but also because the implications for the intellectual property bar are enormous. If this court's decision is upheld by the Supreme Court of California, this would mean that no one could bring a parallel cause of action for unfair competition in any case triable to a jury (including antitrust causes of action, trade secret theft causes of action, etc.) without running the serious risk of losing the right to trial by jury of all those causes of action that are of right triable to a jury.

In the patent laws, it has been determined that where there is an issue of fact that involves both equitable and legal issues, the parties are entitled to have the issue of fact determined by a jury, and the jury's factual determination is binding on the court. This occurs in the willfulness issues where the issue of willfulness is tried to a jury, but the issue of whether to award attorney's fees is up to the court. The court is bound by the jury's findings on willfulness and must take these into consideration in determining whether to award attorney's fees, costs, treble damages, etc.

31

Courtesy, Courtesy, Courtesy

Here is another one of those chapters that has absolutely nothing to do with intellectual property law per se. Nonetheless, this is an issue that is near and dear to my heart, and I have determined that whenever possible I will preach on this particular subject, because it is one that is, in my opinion, of great importance to our profession, not only in terms of how we practice our profession but how we are perceived by the public.

My immediate inspiration for writing this chapter was a conversation I had with my mother about the O.J. Simpson trial wherein she remarked that in spite of all of the fine lawyering that was done in that case (her view, not mine), she was put off by the discourtesy that was shown by the lawyers toward each other, as well as by the commentary of various lawyers talking about the case. As she pointed out, there is no other profession in which its members seem so intent on denigrating other members of the same profession. This lack of courtesy does not merely include the obvious negative and personal remarks that lawyers often make about each other in pleadings as well as to the press; it also includes a style of arguing that one sees repeatedly in pleadings and in oral argument to the court.

I must say that while I do not like to make generalizations, I find this particular style of arguing far more prevalent among relatively inexperienced lawyers than among seasoned practitioners. I believe this may be simply a result of the fact that when we were younger we became caught up in the argument itself and had not yet learned to temper our arguments with wisdom. I am speaking of myself as well, recognizing that I have, in my opinion, evolved from a position where I believed that it was important to make strenuous arguments on every point to a place where I believe that arguments can be made objectively and fairly without resorting to invective and inappropriate characterizations of opponents' arguments.

In my opinion, all lawyers should take a vow to eliminate the following types of phrases from their pleadings and oral arguments: "Incredibly, plaintiff argues that . . ."; "Defendant has lied to the court in representing that . . ."; "Unbelievably, plaintiff would have this court believe that . . ."; "Plaintiff has distorted and misrepresented the facts in this case so as to cause this court to believe that . . ."; "Defendant has engaged in the egregious act of . . ."; and so on.

You get the drift. Every argument that follows these scurrilous introductory phrases can be made just as easily without the phrases as with them. These phrases not only are unprofessional, they raise the ire of opposing counsel and often invite a counterattack that is equally childish. Not only do the lawyers resent these characterizations when directed at them (of course, they think nothing about the impact on opposing counsel when they direct similar barbs), but the judges hate them.

I have many friends who have been unfortunate enough to have been elevated to the federal and state benches, and their constant complaint is the discourtesy shown by lawyers to each other. This kind of conduct is particularly prevalent in discovery disputes, where each side routinely accuses the other of deliberate and willful cover-ups, misrepresentations, hiding evidence, and so on. I know that when I am asked on occasion to review pleadings that lawyers have written in various cases, I am always turned off when I see these kinds of barbarous phrases.

I try assiduously to avoid them in my own pleadings. (It is not often easy to do because, frankly, people sometimes do make arguments that appear to be almost imbecilic, and there is a great temptation to say so. Nonetheless, one should make a conscientious effort to resist characterizing people's arguments in such unflattering terms.) To say that a lawyer is presenting a stupid argument is essentially to say that the lawyer is either stupid or dishonest, or both.

I am constantly amazed when lawyers can be courteous and cooperative on the telephone and then proceed to write pleadings that are insulting and rude. We should, as a profession, attempt to emulate the barristers of England, who are elaborate in their courtesy toward each other, whether it is sincere or not. We should attempt to be more like the Senate, where senators usually bend over backwards to be courteous in addressing each other and in respecting each other's points of view, rather than behaving like the House of Representatives or the British House of Commons, where the latest vogue seems to be to insult each other and call each other's integrity into question.

Any society that promotes rudeness is bound to collapse of its own weight, and we as lawyers should be leaders in the effort to introduce and maintain civility in our courtrooms as well as in our government. I am frankly somewhat surprised that neither our law schools nor the bar teach courtesy as part of their ethics classes.

I am also somewhat surprised at the judiciary, which constantly harangues lawyers about discourtesy, yet never makes any attempt to enforce courtesy by directing the lawyers not to engage in this kind of conduct. It would be helpful if the courts and the bar laid out specific rules governing conduct and courtesy of lawyers toward each other, including prohibiting the use of insulting and accusatory phrases in pleadings and in oral argument. There is nothing that is stated rudely that could not be stated with equal force in a courteous manner. Enough preaching, but I'm writing this book, so I am going to take advantage of this opportunity. You can read it or not, and you can take this advice or disregard it.

If you choose not to read what I have written here, however, or if you should choose to disregard it, then you are a no-good lousy bum, a liar, a thief, and an immoral degenerate (and that's on a good day).[1]

---

1. Incidentally, I have often been guilty of violating my own rule. Recently I dictated a scorching reply memorandum. That evening I decided to redo my work to eliminate the diatribe. Unfortunately, I had emergency surgery so my original went out. In its order, the court took both sides to task for our rhetoric (lesson learned.)

Section 4

Copyrights

32

Copyrights

When Icthiod Ike heard a poem that he liked, he would copy it down with his pen. He would take it home and show it around and sometimes he'd share with his friends.

Now, Icthiod Ike got a terrible fright when he heard from a man named Big Ben.

Big Ben, so it seems, was a man of some means, and a man who owned copyrights.

Big Ben said to Ike, with a scowl on his face, "You're a disgrace to the whole human race."

Icthiod Ike flew into a tizzy. What shall I do? I'll call my friend Lizzy.

Now, Lizzy was fair, she had bright shiny hair and two eyes that twinkled at night.

She was also, it's said, a source of much dread, for Lizzy was not just a hoot.

No, Lizzy, it's said, was that creature of dread, a lawyer of some great repute.

"Oh, Lizzy, I'm doomed," said Icthiod Ike, "for Big Ben will take me to court."

"Don't fret," said Miss Lizzy, "you're acting quite dizzy and there's no need to get out of joint.

"Just change a few words, or the order of such, and you'll find this is not about much."

Now, Icthiod Ike was ecstatic to hear, he would not be thrown out on his ear.

I'll just take these poems and move them around, and I'll smile where I once had a frown.

Alas and alack for Icthiod Ike, for his task was much harder to steer.

For changing the words changed the sound and the feel of the poems he so loved to hear.

So Icthiod Ike turned to Lizzy again, and he said, "Oh tell me, oh what can I do?"

But Lizzy, it seems, was fresh out of schemes, so Ike had to just sit and stew.

For the lesson was clear, that a poem is not words, but the sounds that ring out so clear. It's not just the words, but the way they're composed, that sound so fine in the ear.

Now, Icthiod Ike was incredibly sad, for he knew he could not copy poems. "Oh, what shall I do?" thought Icthiod Ike, "I can't copy and publish the sounds that I like."

He stewed and he fumed and he stomped 'round the house. "I can't copy the poems, the things that I love, without being tagged as a louse." But while lacking in talent, Icthiod Ike was nothing, if he wasn't smart. I can't copy poems, he mused to himself, so I'll copy songs, great books, and fine art.

Returning to Lizzy, he said with a thrill, "My life now has meaning again. I won't copy poems because I cannot, but I'll copy fine songs, great art, and whatnot."

Lizzy shook her head, oh what could she do, her client, it seems, was a hopeless shamoo.

"Icthiod Ike, I know you mean well, but you simply just don't understand. You can't copy music, great books, and fine art, you can't copy them, no, no, you may not."

"Oh how can you say this? How can it be true? My life will be miserable. I'll be nothing but blue."

"Okay! Okay!" sighed the weary Lizzy. "Okay! Okay! We'll work on this biz."

"You can copy your songs, great books, and fine art. You can even copy some poems if you're smart.

"Fair use is the key. Help the public you see. Use all this good stuff educationally.

"So don't be a schnook, put out a book, and include all those fine clever things, created by others to make living a pleasure.

"And throw in your comments, always there for good measure, to give explanation about all this creation.

"Then rather than end up in court,

"You'll be applauded, and all will agree,

"Your efforts we should not abort."

Well, there you have it, a poem by the author. Some of you may have noticed that this was patterned somewhat after a man who has been a great inspiration to us all, Dr. Seuss. While it's not great art, at least it's copyrighted, so don't go copying this and spreading it around like it was your own, or I'll sue you.

That rather pathetic poem was intended to demonstrate a couple of concepts. The first is that copyrights are there to protect creativity. Accordingly, taking the words of a poem and rearranging them so they no longer rhyme destroys the poem, even if you have all the same words. By the same token, taking a book and rewriting it to set forth basically the same ideas, but setting them forth and expressing them in a different manner, is a different creation.

The second principle is that you can use copyrighted material for fair use. In other words, you can take a speech by somebody and include it within a book about that person if you are using the speech to illustrate certain things that that person did in his or her life. That, of course, is just one example; there are many, many others. This is called the "fair use doctrine."

The Most Important Thing to Know About Copyright Law

The most important thing that you can learn about copyright law is to avoid it like the plague. It is confusing; it is complicated; it is difficult; and the only people who care at all about copyrights are Walt Disney (who is now deceased) and the American Bar Association, which wants me to discuss copyrights in this book.

Speaking of Walt Disney reminds me of my childhood. My father was always getting on me for watching cartoons instead of reading law books. Of course, I guess his position was somewhat justified, since I was in law school at the time. Anyway, one afternoon when I was feeling particularly smug, I looked up from a Donald Duck cartoon and queried, "So, who do you think is making more money, you or Walt Disney?"

This simple discussion taught me one of the more valuable lessons that I ever learned as a child: Don't ever win an argument with your parents. The aftermath of that little discussion was enough to make the blood of a grown man run cold. There you have it: That's the most important thing you need to know about copyrights.

33

Other Things You Need to Know About Copyrights

If you follow the generous advice that I have just given you, you won't have to learn anything else about copyrights. While this will not guarantee happiness, it will certainly go a long way toward eliminating a potential source of great unhappiness.

On the assumption that you have ignored my advice (like most of my clients), I guess I have to go on with this subject. The first thing you need to understand is the concept of copyrights. The purpose of a copyright is to protect and encourage creativity. Accordingly, copyright protection usually extends to traditionally creative property such as works of art, songs, books, poems, photographs, essays, movies, plays, and, with the dawn of the new age of technology, computer programs.

Speaking of computer programs, there was a concerted attempt to have the courts extend copyright protection to the look and feel of a program, as was done in the case of *Lotus Development Corporation v. Borland International*, 516 U.S. 233 (1996). The Supreme Court just recently confirmed the fact that the look and feel of a program are not copyrightable. (The decision was 50-50 with no opinion.) I, frankly, don't know why anybody really thought there was a chance of extending the copyright protection to the look and feel of a program in any event, but as of now that whole issue is dead, even though it was greatly exciting to a few people whose lives are otherwise hopelessly boring.

Other areas subject to copyright protection are cartoon characters (which are jealously guarded and rigorously enforced by companies such as Disney) and the personal identities of celebrities. The latter is a relatively recent development in the law and one of which I disapprove (like who cares whether I approve or not); it just seems that these people have enough going for them without getting special protection under the law.

Of course, the development of the Internet is wreaking havoc and letting loose the gods of war in the field of copyright law. All this downloading is giving copyright lawyers monstrous headaches, resulting in increasingly nasty dispositions.

Also, piracy of records, tapes, CDs, movies, and the like is big business and keeps a lot of copyright lawyers' children in college. It is also responsible for copyright lawyers' children getting braces and other necessary dental work, and even some occasional cosmetic surgery. This type of thing is what keeps dentists and surgeons happy and prosperous, thereby moving money throughout the economy and helping to raise all boats. At the risk of being sued for copyright infringement myself, I must quote from a famous man (whose name I don't remember), who said that "a rising tide casts a silver lining over all the boats that rise at once." Actually I think that's an amalgam of quotes, and I think I'll copyright it myself.

As long as we are digressing, as is my wont, let me ask you a question. Who out there knows what were the two greatest problems in Beethoven's life? Give up? The answers are first, having to deal with his good-for-nothing nephew who was always hitting him up for cash, and second, trying to convince his publisher to protect his copyrights. And you thought Beethoven had nothing to teach you.

How do you enforce a copyright? Well, obviously, the first thing you could do is to obtain an injunction. This is the relief most often sought in these cases because of the difficulty of establishing damages, which we will discuss a little later.

Since so many of these copyright cases involve willful infringement, piracy, and importing of illegal copyrighted materials by bandits and such, a popular means of enforcement is a predawn raid by U.S. marshals pursuant to a TRO obtained through an ex parte emergency proceeding. Since this kind of copyright infringement is a federal crime as well, the lawyer instituting the raid should also notify the district attorney's office or the FBI or some such.

The great advantage of these raids, of course, is that they do not allow the crook time to escape on the back of a flatbed truck to avoid the jurisdiction of the court. The disadvantage is that if you blow it and wrongly accuse somebody, you may be faced with a suit for malicious prosecution and other unpleasantness. We discussed a similar situation in the area of trademark enforcement.

Now, you may recall I said to stay clear of this area of the law. Among my many good reasons for making this suggestion is that, unless you are representing a big company like Disney, which is very intent on protecting its copyrighted materials, there is not a whole lot of money in it. By that I mean it's hard to prove and establish substantial damages.

Under the copyright laws, you are entitled to a reasonable royalty on each copyrighted sale, which may be a mere pittance if the sales of the copyrighted material are not of a substantial dollar amount. Since potentially successful copyright infringement is usually nipped in the bud by an injunction, there usually is not a substantial accrual of royalty sales. (Of course, there are exceptions, particularly involving hit songs, movies, etc.)

Congress, not being composed entirely of fools (just kidding, of course), in its infinite wisdom, provided an alternate means of obtaining compensation. It has provided for a per-infringement penalty that can be sought as an alternative. Now, this sounds like a pretty good deal. You figure some guy goes out and publishes 25,000 copies of your client's photo essays and sells them for 50 cents apiece. Now, looking at royalties, this does not look like a lot of money, but when you figure you are going to get paid a fee on each item of infringement, you whip out your calculator and calculate the fee times 25,000 and you start figuring that the money is going to mount up. Right? Wrong. Why not? Because. (In case you haven't noticed by now, "because," as in "Because I told you so," is the perfect answer to virtually any question. Another lesson I learned from my parents.)

The answer is because the courts have held that the penalty per publication does not refer to each individual item published, but rather to each run of the press or each issue. So, if *Time* magazine infringes your client's copyright in its April edition, that would be considered one publication for purposes of the penalty part of the statute.

I once tried a case in Connecticut involving the Rubik's Cube (*Abeshouse v. Ultragraphics*, 754 F.2d 467 (1985)). In that case, my clients, who were artists, had worked with a Yale math professor who had developed a solution to the Rubik's Cube. Together they designed a poster showing the solution. Being of a clever bent, my clients had obtained a copyright on their poster, of which they were rightfully quite proud.

Thereafter, they entered into an agreement with a company (it was actually a sole proprietorship and they dealt with the proprietor—who else?) to print copies of their posters and sell them. This he proceeded to do and paid them the agreed-on royalty. Unfortunately, my clients had a falling out with this printer (who wasn't actually a printer at all, but was jobbing the posters out and acting as the salesperson). As a result of their falling out, my clients decided to no longer do business with this individual (which they had a right to do) and to secure the services of another. Now, this sales agent/printer/whatever else was very disconcerted by my clients' decision because he had all kinds of potential orders from potential customers. Accordingly, he justified to himself printing these posters on his own, without the awkward necessity of informing my clients, and distributing them to all of these customers throughout the United States and Europe. To avoid any charges of copyright infringement, he developed the ingenious notion of simply removing my clients' copyright notation.

The jury did not think much of this rationale and ended up awarding my clients approximately twice as much as we asked. Unfortunately, the Second Circuit was not impressed with the poetic justice rendered by the jury and ordered either a new trial or a remittitur in the alternative.

Even though we had an open-and-shut case of copyright infringement, we were not able to build up a damage case the way I would have liked because the sales dollar amount was not that great, and the penalty alternative was limited to a small number of publications because the posters were printed in a limited number of lots.

The other reason to avoid copyright law like the plague is because of the confusion about the length of time of copyrights. Relatively recent changes in the copyright law have changed the time for the existence of a copyright. That time extension, however, only extends to copyrights published after a certain date. The time periods are calculated based on the life of the author in a manner reminiscent of the rule against perpetuities, the bane of every law student's existence. We are not going to get into the time period extended to copyrights because, frankly, that is a subject better left to a discourse on wills and estates.

Okay, okay, you don't believe me. You think that I just don't want to give you this extremely valuable information. All right, let me show you what I mean.

First of all, for works published after 1978, things are pretty simple. The duration of a copyright for a single author, not for hire, is 50 years from the end of the year of the date of death of the author. In other words, if the author were to die in June 1980, then the copyright would end 50 years from December 31, 1980. In the event the date of death of the author is unknown, then the copyright expires either 75 years from the date of publication or 100 years from the date of creation, whichever is longer. There are provisions for notifying the Patent Office and filing information about the date of death or lack thereof, and so on and so on, that we do not need to get into in detail at this time. One item of interest is that if a person relies on the 75- or 100-year date and it turns out that it was wrong, that the author lived to a ripe old age and the 75- or 100-year time periods were less than his date of death plus 50 years, that 100-year provision is available as a defense to the person who reasonably relied on it, *but it would not be available to those who found out the truth later.*

You may be asking yourself, "What is the difference between a date of publication and date of creation, and why do we have these different provisions?" This is why I said that this area is better left to a discussion on wills and estates (actually, it is only one of the reasons but it is a pretty good one). This 100-year provision covers a situation where your client inherited a bunch of old beaten-up manuscripts, which were written by her brilliant but horribly shy great-uncle, who wrote all of his poems on notebook paper but never showed them to anyone. Since they were never published, arguably, there should be no restriction as to when they entered the public domain, since almost all copyright laws stem from the date of publication. There is a provision in the Constitution, however, that limits copyright protection to some reasonable amount of time, and therefore, the legislature has arbitrarily decreed 100 years from the date of creation as sort of a nice little compromise.

What about a work made for hire? We will discuss works made for hire a little later, but it is a pretty simple concept. If you work for someone and you do something for them as part of your employment, your work belongs to them. (I have already told you what is going to be in the next chapter, so you can ignore it.) It makes little sense to talk about death where a work made for hire is concerned, particularly where the employer is a corporation. Therefore, Congress has decided to use the 75- and 100-year time periods in the following manner: The duration of a copyright, of a work made for hire, is either 100 years from the date of its creation or 75 years from the date of its publication, whichever is longer.

Another issue that occasionally arises is what happens in the case of joint authors. In the joint authors situation, the life plus 50 years is determined by whoever lives the longest. Sometimes, people actually pretend to have co-authored a document with a much younger person, to fraudulently extend the life of the copyright. Why a lot of people worry so much about what is going to happen after they are dead and gone is a philosophical question that has probably been explored by greater philosophers than the author.

So you are probably asking yourself. "Why all the fuss?" You are most likely saying, "This seems pretty straightforward and I do not know why this should be difficult for anyone to follow." The answer lies not with the present state of the law, but in what went on before.

The present time periods that we have discussed above were passed for a number of reasons, not the least of which was to set the groundwork for the United States to become a signatory to the Berne Convention, which it finally did in 1988, 12 years after the passage of the present copyright statute. The time periods that we just discussed bring the United States in line with the other signatories to the Berne Convention. There are a number of other aspects to the Berne Convention, and if you are really dealing with international copyright law, I suggest you study it in detail. Since this is not a treatise on international copyright law, we are not going to become heavily involved in that discussion. (As an observational note, I can recall a time when the Berne Convention was considered to be somewhat akin to a communist plot or some grim plan by the United Nations as part of its overall scheme to take over the United States military. Fortunately, we have gone beyond that period of national paranoia, and intellectual property law is rapidly becoming a full-blown area of international law, reflective of the current international state of interdependence of economies throughout the world. But I digress again.)

So let's return to that part of the copyright law that has made it a major mess in the past and that makes this a subject better suited to wills and estates. In particular, what I am referring to is the copyright renewal provision that existed in the law until the effective date of the present copyright law of 1978. (It was passed in 1976 and effective in 1978.) As you saw above, the present copyright term period is pretty straightforward and neat and clean, assuming that we can figure out when a person died and things of that nature. The old law (1909 and actually every law preceding that, going back to the 1700s) provided for a limited copyright period, such as 28 years, and the opportunity for renewals thereafter. We are still stuck with all this renewal business for works created before 1978. Fortunately, with each passing year, we have fewer and fewer related problems in this area. Just to give you an example of how complicated that particular area of the law was (or is), I have pulled out my handy volume of *Nimmer on Copyright*. (If you are at all serious about copyright law, you absolutely have to have *Nimmer on Copyright* in your library. To do otherwise is not only bad form but is indicative of questionably subversive political leanings. A truly patriotic American who is interested in copyright law will always have *Nimmer on Copyright* in his or her library.)

Section 9.02 of Volume 2, Nimmer quotes from the congressional history of the 102d Congress (1991) condemning the renewal provision of the 1976 act—it is itself copied from the identical section of the 1909 act—as "a highly technical provision which is *too difficult for most lawyers to understand*. Its effects are felt most harshly by the holders of a copyright in less noted works who typically lack the sophisticated resources . . . to keep track of renewal dates or the services of lawyers, agents and large publishing houses—to assist them in complying with the intricacies of the renewal provision" (emphasis added). Amen to that! The headings and subheadings of Nimmer's discussion on the renewal provision include the following:

- The Rationale of the Renewal Concept
- Works in Which Copyright Renewals Vest in Proprietors
- Posthumous Works
- Composite Works
- Works Copyrighted by a Corporate Body Otherwise Than as Assignee or Licensee of the Individual Author
- Works Copyrighted by an Employer for Hire
- Renewal Rights in the Author and Successor Classes
- The Widow (Widower) and Children
- Division Within the Widow-Children Class
- The Meaning of "Children" Within the Class
- The Meaning of "Widow"
- The Author's Executors
- The Author's Next of Kin
- The Process of Renewal
- Introduction
- Renewal of Works That Obtained Statutory Copyright before 1964
- Renewal of Works That Obtained Statutory Copyright from 1964 to 1977

Treatment of Restored Copyrights

- When the Renewal Copyright Must Be Registered
- 1964–1977 Works
- Vesting of Renewal Interests
- When the Renewal Copyright Vests
- In Whom Renewal Vests
- Renewal Registration
- Renewal Claimants
- Renewal Certificates as Prima Facie Evidence
- Renewal Formalities for Joint Works
- Renewal Formalities Under the Multilateral Conventions

- Grants of Renewal Rights
- Construction of Grants Which Do Not Expressly Mention Renewal Rights
- When a Transfer of Renewal Rights Will Be Valid and Enforceable as Against the Transferor
- The Value of Renewal Rights to Authors
- The Effect of an Unconscionable Assignment
- The Effect of an Assignment of Renewal Rights by Co-Owners When Such Rights Do Not Vest in All of the Co-Owners
- The Effect of a Transfer of Renewal Rights When the Transferor Does Not Survive Until Renewal Vests
- Transfer of a Renewal Expectancy Which Will Vest in the Copyright Proprietor
- Extraterritorial Effect of United States Reversion of Renewal
- The Effect of a Termination of Rights After the Original Term of Copyright upon Previously Created Copies and Derivative Works

Are you convinced yet? If you are really interested in any of the topics that have just been set forth above, this indicates one of a number of considerations:

1. You really have no life.
2. You have a life but you are really not satisfied with it.
3. You are a distant cousin of Mr. Nimmer.
4. You have an estate practice with some really strange clients who have inherited no money but somehow have obtained a bunch of dusty old unpublished manuscripts that they somehow think are worth a lot of money.
5. You have a burning desire to know everything there is to know about a totally unintelligible area of the law, and therefore you are beyond any hope of salvation.

In any event, if you really want any detailed information on a very real copyright problem, then just pull out *Nimmer* and you will undoubtedly find your answer.

Copyrights do not have to be registered to be protected. All you have to do to protect the copyright is put a little *c* within a circle, followed by the year and your name, and then publish it. You can publish it by making copies and mailing them to your friends. You can also obtain a registered copyright. One of the advantages of a registered copyright is that when it is infringed, you can obtain attorney's fees. It also makes it easier to establish your copyright and to establish the probable infringement by the person you wish to sue.

Incidentally, to establish copyright infringement, you have to establish not only that the accused publication is substantially similar to the copyrighted material but that the material was actually copied. This does not have to be proven by direct evidence; it can be inferred by circumstantial evidence. Usually the best evidence is to establish the accessibility to the accused of the copyrighted material.

In copyright suits involving music there is often an issue of substantial similarity because often there are overlappings between various notes, chords, etc., of legitimately different works. If an accused work is substantially similar (a jury question) to the copyrighted work and if the jury believes there was access to the material, then the jury can find infringement.

Now, you might be saying, "How could access be a problem if the copyrighted material is registered with the Library of Congress?" Well, one defense is that the accused material was actually developed by the accused infringer subsequent to the creation of the copyrighted work but prior to its registration or publication. Another argument is that it was developed in a foreign country, where the accused infringer was not aware of its existence or registration, and then brought into this country. These are jury questions, and they sometimes yield results that are very disconcerting to both parties. (So what's new?)

Finally, I've reminded myself of one other area of copyrightable material, and that is in the area of game boards. If you recall, when we discussed the Monopoly situation under trademarks, we talked about how Monopoly lost its trademark. This did not mean, however, that it would lose its copyrights on the artwork on the game board itself. When I first started practicing patent law, I knew a patent lawyer who spent his spare time designing game boards and games. He would copyright the game boards and patent the games and then spend the rest of his time trying to find someone who gave a darn. He was never successful in interesting anybody in any of his work, which once again establishes the wisdom of Thomas Jefferson, a wise American, who was best known and remembered for stating, "Patent lawyers should stay at home and watch more television, damn it!"

Fair Use Doctrine (Copyrights)

We have already discussed fair use briefly in my neat, Dr. Seussian-type poem.

It should be fairly obvious to you just from having lived on this planet (lawyers and other creatures from distant planets should ignore this section) that people are always quoting other people's works or incorporating them by reference in publications, movies, speeches, etc. For example, a person writing a book about Abraham Lincoln would be expected to quote rather extensively from Abraham Lincoln's speeches. If those speeches were copyrighted and the copyrights were extant today, a person writing such a biography would still have the right to take excerpts from the speeches.

Because there is no hard-and-fast rule as to how much can be copied, this is often a source of controversy. People whose works are copyrighted frequently will complain that someone's asserted fair use of their works is nothing more than impermissible violation of their copyright rights. This is the kind of question that becomes an issue for the trier of fact and is one the reasons why there are lawsuits and why lawyers have jobs. It is these kinds of uncertainties in the law that cause people to accuse lawyers of writing laws to suit their own profession. Actually that's not true. The laws simply reflect the ambiguities of life in general.

The cases and examples of fair use are extensive and have been discussed at length in far more impressive intellectual property discourses than are ever going to be presented in this text. Nonetheless, this should give you some fundamental insight into the fact that such a doctrine exists and that it is an important concept in intellectual property law. See, for example, *Campbell v. Acuff-Rose Music*, 510 U.S. 569 (1994), for a good discussion of this principle. An important area relating to the impact of fair use on the modern world is fair use of software.

It has been held that one may reproduce software for the purpose of designing around it. This is true, even if the designing around is for a commercial purpose. Probably the most important case regarding that issue is *Atari Games Corp. vs. Nintendo of America, Inc.*, 9785 Fed.2d, 832, 843 (Fed. Cir. 1992). This is consistent with the decisions in *Bateman vs. Mnemonics, Inc.*, 79 Fed.3d, 1532, 1539, n.18 (11th Cir. 1986) and *Sega Enters., Ltd. vs. Accolade, Inc.*, 977 Fed.2d, 1510, 1527-28 (9th Cir. 1992).

Loss of Copyright Protection

It used to be the law that if you ever published any material without affixing a copyright designation, you would have waived your copyright rights forever. That harsh result was changed not too many years ago so that the publication of material without the copyright designation does not necessarily terminate one's copyright rights altogether. Of course, anyone who does publish your material before you have designated it as copyrighted and/or registered may do so at will without fear of being accused of copyright infringement.

If one later decides to publish material that has been published without a copyright notation for a limited period of time, that person may do so, provided there has been proper notification given to those who have most likely received copies of the material before it was copyrighted or designated as copyrighted. Obviously, to be on the safe side, nothing should be published without the copyright designation, and the copyright should be registered as soon as possible.

How to Register a Copyright

To register a copyright, simply get a form from the Library of Congress, fill in the blanks, and send in the form with a check and the appropriate number of copies of your material. The rest, as they say, is history.

For software, always make sure you pay attention to paragraph 6—contributions of others. Most programs contain many off-the-shelf modules. Failure to reference them may invalidate a copyright or even subject your client to an allegation of fraud on the copyright office.

Works Made for Hire (Copyrights)

If a person is an independent contractor and is hired to create a work of art, then the copyright rights for that art belong to that person. This issue often arises where photographs are concerned. A person who hires a photographer to take neat celebrity pictures of the subject and the subject's family may be surprised to discover those same photographs appearing somewhere in a book copyrighted by the photographer. This is the photographer's right, absent some expressed contractual provision to the contrary. The person who paid to have the photographs taken has a right only to the photographs that he purchased. Of course, theoretically there could be some right to privacy being infringed, depending on the use that is made of the photographs, but the copyright to the photographs belongs with the photographer.

The second area where this type of thing often arises is where someone is an in-house employee whose job it is to write books, make photographs, etc. That person has no independent copyrights. Those rights belong to the employer. (This is similar to the situation in patents, where an employee whose job it is to develop products has no independent ownership rights in the patents made while an employee.)

Software Copyrights

We have already discussed software copyright litigation, particularly as it relates to counterclaims. At this time, I would like to flesh out, in a little more detail, what is involved in software copyrights in general.

A popular misconception is that anyone can simply write a computer program, take it down to the Library of Congress, file for copyright registration, and thereby protect the entire program. That is simply not the law. Most copyrighted programs, even those that contain some protectable copyright material, will also contain a substantial portion that is not copyrightable for a variety of reasons. The most common reason is that the software incorporates a lot of other existing copyrighted programs that either belong to someone else or are not copyrightable. In any event, they are not copyrightable by the person seeking to copyright his or her unique contribution. It is only the unique portion of the program that is subject to copyright protection. Accordingly, when one files a computer program, one is required to submit the first and last 25 pages of the copyrightable portion of the program.

It should be noted that one of the disadvantages of filing for copyright protection is that the public then has access to those portions of the copyrighted program that have been filed. This may make it possible for someone wishing to copy the program to have an opportunity to have a "leg up" in this regard. If the person copying the program intends it for private use only, it may be difficult, if not impossible, to catch him or her at it.[1]

What is definitely not copyrightable is a computer program that is

---

1. There is a provision for deleting trade secret portions of the program, but this may be of limited practical value.

essential to utility. In other words, if the purpose and objective to be obtained by the copyright dictates that the program be written in a certain manner and in that manner only, then that program is not copyright-protectable. The reason is that copyrights are intended to protect creativity and means of expression. If the program is entirely functional, there is no expression involved. In other words, the only way that one can obtain copyright protectability relating to function is if there are a number of ways the software could be written and still obtain the same functionality.

In many cases, copyright infringement is not readily contestable because the accused infringer has taken a program, which it has often purchased, and simply downloaded it on a number of additional computers, thereby engaging in unauthorized use of the program. Once the evidence has established that some unauthorized use has occurred, the case is usually made, except for the defense that the material was not subject to copyright protection in the first place.

The extremely difficult cases to prove are those in which someone is accused of writing their own programs, but, in the course of doing so, copying the copyrighted material of the plaintiff's registered software copyright. In order to prove those cases, it is usually necessary to obtain copies of the defendant's source code, or its object code, and compare the two. This is often difficult, if not impossible.

In order to establish copyright infringement, it is not always necessary to establish a one-to-one or literal copying of the copyrighted code. For example, one might also establish copyright infringement by showing an identity of the screen output coupled with showing that the structure and organization of the two programs are essentially the same. Of course, showing that the structure and organization are the same requires a comparison of the two programs. I am presently involved in a case where the plaintiff is attempting to establish copyright infringement by showing that there are some similarities between some items found on the screens of the copyrighted software and the screens of the accused software. In my opinion, that case has no chance of success, and our motion for summary judgment is pending.

It should be noted that there is a substantial body of law holding that even if the screens are identical, that does not necessarily mean that the programs are identical. One can use different programs to achieve the same screen output. In light of this law, the fact that there are some similarities of some items (all of which relate to function) between copyrighted software and another person's software should be of no significance whatsoever in establishing copyright infringement. It should also be noted in that case that there was never an attempt to actually compare software to software, and no attempt to establish identity or even similarity of structure, organization, etc.

Finally, and perhaps most important, one cannot obtain a software copyright on material created by another. As I indicated previously, the filing of such a software application and thereafter attempting to enforce such registration could result in a counterclaim based upon fraud on the copyright office.

34

Potential Pitfalls from Those Pesky Presumptions

I recently had a close call that dramatically illustrated my two favorite platitudes: first, that a little knowledge is a dangerous thing; second, you have to watch these judges like a hawk.

The case was one for copyright infringement. The plaintiff had filed a motion for preliminary injunction, and I, on behalf of the defendant, had filed a cross-motion for summary judgment of noninfringement and copyright invalidity. At the beginning of the hearing, the court announced that because copyright invalidity had not been affirmatively pled as a defense, he had no jurisdiction to decide that issue. The court's statement took me completely by surprise because the other side had not raised that issue. Because I was surprised, I sat mute and was thinking that I would have to seek leave of court to file an amended answer. The court then went on to begin a discussion of other matters when my brain finally clicked from the off position to the on position. I timidly raised my hand and said, "Excuse me all to pieces for interrupting Your Honor, sir, but the statement you just made is dead wrong." The judge's mouth dropped open and he glared at me with two beady eyes from which emitted two laser beams that burned themselves into my tender skull. "What's that you say?" snarled the judge. "Well," I mumbled almost incoherently, "you see, Your Honor, sir, a copyright registration merely raises a presumption of copyright validity. That presumption, however, disappears as soon as any evidence is introduced that calls into question the validity of the copyright. The ultimate burden of establishing copyright validity rests with the copyright holder. Accord-

183

ingly, once any evidence is introduced that calls into question the validity of the copyright registration, the burden shifts to the plaintiff, and the plaintiff must then establish copyright validity as an element of its case."

A few seconds passed while the color of the smoke emanating from the judge's ears changed from a pleasant white to an unpleasant black. "That shows how much you know," the judge snarled. "I just finished trying a patent case where patent invalidity had to be pled as an affirmative defense and had to be proved by the defendant."

At that point I was so upset, I had to leave the room. Fortunately, my client was well grounded in the intricacies of intellectual property law and was able to proceed quite nicely without me. "If Mr. O'Connor were still in the room, your Honor, I'm sure he would say the following: Yes, it's true that in a patent case the presumption of validity exists throughout the trial and the burden of establishing invalidity lies with the defendant, who must plead patent invalidity as an affirmative defense and who thereby carries the burden of proving such invalidity. And that is because, before a patent can issue, it has to be rigorously examined by one skilled in the art. A copyright registration, on the other hand, is obtained merely by the filing of a form and meeting the requirements of the copyright office. Copyright applications are only examined to make sure that they meet the requirements for a filing of a copyright registration. There is no independent examination of a copyright to determine if the person seeking a copyright is actually entitled to a copyright. And the presumption of copyright validity is based on nothing more than the representations made to the copyright office by the applicant. Accordingly, unlike in the case with a patent, the burden of proving copyright validity ultimately lies with the copyright holder, and there is no requirement or obligation on the part of the defendant to affirmatively plead the copyright invalidity and no requirement that copyright invalidity be proven." We then cited a number of cases, including the following: *Feist Publications, Inc. v. Rural Telephone Service Co., Inc.*, 499 U.S. 340, 345 (Dist. Colo. 1991); *Russ Berrie & Company v. Jerry Elsner Co., Inc.*, 482 F. Supp 980, 988 (S.D.N.Y. 1980); *Whimsicality, Inc. v. Rubie's Costume Co., Inc.*, 891 F.2d 452, 456 (2d Cir. 1989); *Tom Martin d/b/a Martin Creative et al. v. Richard J. Cuny, Benchmark Liquors, Inc.*, 887 F. Supp. 1390, 1394 (Dist. Colo. 1995); *Entertainment Research Group, Inc. v. Genesis Creative Group, Inc. et al.*, 122 F.3d 1211, 1217–19 (9th Cir. 1997); *Fred Riley Home Building Corporation, Bonnie's Designs, Inc., etc., et al. v. Charles Cosgrove d/b/a/ Traditional Homes, et al.*, 883 F. Supp. 1478 (Dist. Kan. 1995).

At that point, the judge decided that I could be readmitted to his courtroom. He has taken the matter under advisement. The lesson for me was, "When in doubt, plead it."

35

Cybersquatting

Some of you may recall that a few years back it was a common practice in a number of Latin American countries for individuals to obtain trademark registration on well-known names, such as Coca-Cola. The owners of those registrations then attempted to essentially blackmail major U.S. corporations into paying them exorbitant fees to obtain the use of their own trademarks. This practice has widely disappeared and is no longer allowed in Latin America.

Somewhat similarly, a number of companies engaged in the practice of trading on the goodwill of known trademarks for products unrelated to those covered by the registered trademarks. That practice is now prohibited in this country, and a person who is improperly using a trademark, even if it is for an unrelated class of goods or services, can be enjoined, and damages can be obtained for the unauthorized and improper use of the registered mark. This is called dilution.

Not surprisingly, ingenious entrepreneurs decided to embark on a similar course of conduct regarding the Internet. It was common for individuals to register domain names that incorporated well-known trademarks. Since the person obtaining the domain name registration was not selling any products, they could not be sued for trading off the goodwill of a registered mark, nor could they be sued for trademark infringement. These individuals became affectionately known as "cybersquatters."

To deal with that clearly unconscionable behavior, Congress passed a cybersquatting law making such domain registrations illegal. It provided for injunction as well as for damages. An interesting constitutional issue (which to date has been noticed by no one other than your modest author) relates to the ex post facto application of the cybersquatting law. The law provides that it reaches back to registrations that were obtained prior to the passage of the legislation. A person who obtained a registration of a mark in violation of the cybersquatting law can be enjoined from using that mark, even if the domain name registration was obtained before the passage of the legislation.

While such a provision would appear to be eminently fair, it also appears, to me at least, to be eminently unconstitutional. For those interested in reading the Constitution (instead of constantly inaccurately paraphrasing it), there is a provision that prohibits government interference with the obligation of a contract. If an Internet provider has contracted with an individual to register a certain domain name, it would appear that the ex post facto application of the anticybersquatting law would be an interference with an obligation of contract. To date, to my knowledge, no one has raised that issue, nor has anyone asked me to raise it. Accordingly, you can probably feel safe to forget what I've said because it is of no relevance in any event.[1]

---

1. That's probably true of this entire book.

36

Can the Late Sonny Bono Save Mickey Mouse?

The Sonny Bono amendment to the copyright laws extended the term of a copyright for 20 years. As of this writing, the Supreme Court has heard oral argument on the question of whether that extension was legal and constitutional or whether it was an inappropriate use of congressional power. As you are reading this chapter, that decision has already been made. Accordingly, you now know more about that issue than I do.[1]

---

1. The decision has now come down. Mickey Mouse won—but—don't expect another extension or if another extension is passed, don't expect it to survive the courts. The Constitution provides limited (in time) protection.

Section 5

Putting It All Together

37

The Inkjet Aftermarket: What It Means to Repair/Reconstruction—and What Does This Have to Do With the Digital Millennium Copyright Act?

A few years ago I became involved in the inkjet aftermarket in a case entitled *Hewlett-Packard vs. Repeat-O-Type Stencil Mfg. Corp., Inc.*, 123 Fed.3d 1445 (Fed. Cir. 1997).

That was a case in which Hewlett-Packard sued Repeat-O-Type for infringement of multiple patents. My client, Repeat-O-Type, was purchasing new Hewlett-Packard black ink cartridges. It was then removing the Hewlett-Packard black ink and replacing that ink with colored ink of its own.

Hewlett-Packard's position was that the removal and replacement of its ink with Repeat-O-Type ink was patent infringement, because the Hewlett-Packard cartridges were not intended to be used in that fashion, and that by removing and replacing the ink, Repeat-O-Type had created a new product in violation of the patent law's prohibition on making an infringing product.

We filed for summary judgment on the basis that Hewlett-Packard's patent rights were extinguished upon the first sale of their products and that Repeat-O-Type had an absolute right to remove and replace ink. In addition, it was our position that if the patents covered anything at all (and there was a real question as to whether they did), they would only cover the structure of the cartridges. There were no claim elements that included the ink. Accordingly, the entire Hewlett-Packard product would not have been covered by any patents, if that product were construed to be the containers filled with Hewlett-Packard ink. The court agreed and granted summary judgment in our behalf. Hewlett-Packard appealed. The Court of Appeals for the Federal Circuit affirmed the lower court's decision and held that what Repeat-O-Type was doing was closer to repair than reconstruction.

Frankly, while we were extremely pleased with the results, we were somewhat surprised by the opinion. In fact, it was our position that the case had nothing to do with the repair/reconstruction doctrine because nothing was being repaired nor reconstructed. It was simply a matter of using the cartridges in a manner in which the purchaser of the cartridges had every right to use them. Hewlett-Packard freely admitted that a purchaser of their ink cartridges had every right to refill those cartridges with other inks. Hewlett-Packard's apparent grievance, in this regard, had to do with the fact that Repeat-O-Type was doing so for commercial reasons.

The fundamental doctrine of repair/reconstruction was enunciated by the U.S. Supreme Court in *Aro Manufacturing v. Convertible Top Replacement*, 377 U.S. 476 (1964). That case involved a plaintiff that had a patent on convertible tops for automobiles. The defendant was a company that replaced the canvas tops on those convertibles when they wore out. The Supreme Court held that this was permissible repair and not complete reconstruction, which would violate the patent prohibition against making the product. As far as I know, there have been no cases in this or the last century that have found a refurbishing of a used product to be a reconstruction in violation of the patent laws. The only case of which I am aware was a case sometime in the 1800s involving baling wire and some sort of metal strap with a buckle (if my recollection is correct). In that case, the defendant found pieces of the straps in a junkyard, soldered them together, and essentially made a new product from scrap metal.

So, why is this case significant? It is significant because there is a substantial aftermarket for refurbished products and for refilling of ink into products such as those made by Hewlett-Packard, Canon, etc.

You may have noted that the title to this chapter includes a reference to the Digital Millennium Copyright Act, 17 U.S.C. § 1201 et seq. The reason I put that statute into this section is because of *Lexmark vs. Static Control,* presently pending in the Eastern District of Kentucky.

Lexmark makes toner cartridges that include a microchip containing a copyrighted program used to determine toner levels in the cartridge. Located on a controller board inside the Lexmark Laser Printers is a Printer Engine Program that controls various printer operations. Lexmark uses a technological measure to prevent unauthorized access to its programs by means of a special communication between the microchip on the cartridges and the printer. If the microchip and the printer communicate properly, the printer recognizes that the toner cartridge is authorized and printer functionality is enabled.

Static Control makes and sells components to the toner cartridge remanufacturing industry, which allows consumers to circumvent the Lexmark chip and refill and reuse the cartridges without returning them to Lexmark. Lexmark sued on the basis of the Digital Millennium Copyright Act. That act essentially provides civil as well as criminal penalties to those who market technology that can be used to circumvent the technology created to prevent copying of copyrighted material such as software programs.

Static Control's probable defense (if I may speak for them—and they have never given me permission to do so) is that their product has nothing to do with the copying of the software in the Lexmark products. Their product is only intended to allow a person to circumvent technology that would prohibit the use of the Lexmark product.

At present, that case is very much up in the air, and ultimately the decision of what is encompassed by this statute will probably have to be decided by the Supreme Court.

In *United States v. ELCOMLTD Etc.*, 203 F. Supp. 2d 1111 (Northern District of California), the court upheld the constitutionality of the Digital Millennium Copyright Act as it applied to a criminal indictment. That particular decision was a very thoroughly researched and well-written opinion by Judge Ronald M. Whyte, and I recommend it to anyone who is interested in a thorough and careful analysis of that statute.

Of course, that statute was not specifically designed and intended to be applicable to the ink aftermarket products. Nonetheless, its applicability to such products in the *Lexmark* case is an interesting evolution in the law (including repair/reconstruction) as it relates to this area of the law, which portends to be one of great judicial ferment.

38

License Agreements Regarding Standing to Sue

This can be tricky, and we are not going into detail here, as licensing is its own field of specialization. Suffice it to say that an assignment of a patent gives standing to the assignee to sue. An exclusive license may give standing, but may require joinder of the inventor. A non-exclusive usually does not give standing, but might with joinder of the inventor.

I hate to be so vague (actually, I enjoy it), but so much depends on the actual wording of the technology transfer document. It is difficult to make accurate generalizations.

We had a case where the assignee specifically was assigned the right to sue. The court found that, in fact, it was a non-exclusive license because the inventor wasn't initially joined (he later joined, but it was too late). The assignee had no standing and we obtained summary judgment. The right to sue was for two years only, and the summary judgment was entered after the two years. Result: one out-of-luck and very angry plaintiff.

Be sure to consult a specialist when entering into any patent license agreement, and make sure you discuss all the possible ramifications of potential litigation.

39

What Are the Biggest Evidentiary Loopholes in Intellectual Property Litigation?

When I was in high school, I was in a play called "The Gazebo." One of my lines was something like, "If I can't goes under, I goes through. If I can't goes through, I goes around. Now, where's the body, Mr. Nash?"

After the play, my father asked me if I learned anything from my part. I answered, "Sure did. Mafiosos wear the coolest clothes."

It wasn't until I'd been practicing law for some 30 years that it hit me. In law, as in life, there is more than one way to skin a cat.[1] If you can't get evidence in on one theory, use another. The biggest loophole—state of mind, intent, malice. Think about it. I'm not spoon-feeding all the answers here.

The second biggest loophole is using an expert to testify that he or she "relied" on all kinds of inadmissible stuff in formulating an opinion.

The most effective objection is lack of foundation. There is nothing more pathetic than a lawyer who can't present a prima facie case because the key witness can't establish a proper foundation for essential testimony. Most people think they know things they actually don't know at all. This may be ok in life, but it is deadly in the courtroom.

---

1. What a ghastly expression. Who comes up with these things, anyway?

40

Design Patents, Copyrights, and Trademarks

We have already discussed design patents, copyrights, and trademarks in other parts of this book. I decided, however, to throw in a little section discussing all three of them together because often there is confusion about the similarities, overlaps, and differences among and between these kinds of protection.

In the first place, there can be overlaps. For example, one can have a copyright on a cartoon character and also use that cartoon character as a trademark for certain products.

One can also have a design patent and a copyright on the same image. For example, one could have a copyright on a sculpture and a design patent on an ashtray in the shape of that sculpture. One can also use the image of that sculpture as a trademark. All three types of intellectual property protection have different means of enforcement, different time periods of protection, and different and distinct remedies.

Know this and be wise.

41

Caveat

In case you haven't noticed by now, this book was not intended to be a research book. It is intended to give you an introduction to intellectual property law and to give you a flavor and a sense of the kinds of issues that one encounters. This is not a thorough and complete text and should not be viewed as such.

An example of why this is a subject for only the certifiably insane can be demonstrated by the following situation that I actually encountered. Ask yourself the following questions: If an inventor has filed a patent application in the United States and filed a corresponding foreign application pursuant to one of the various treaties (such as the Patent Cooperation Treaty sponsored by the United Nations), and the foreign application is in a country that follows the procedure of publishing patent applications before their issuance, and if the inventor subsequently files a continuation-in-part of the U.S. application using the original filing date of the original application as the filing date for the continuation-in-part, and also files the same continuation-in-part in the foreign country more than a year after the publication of the original patent application in the foreign country, does the foreign country's publication of the original patent application in the foreign country serve as prior art to the continuation-in-part in the United States? Does it serve as prior art to the continuation-in-part in the foreign country?

I am not going to give you the answers to those questions, because if you really want to know the answers, then you are a patent lawyer and you are beyond all hope of redemption. I merely posed these questions to give you an idea of the esoteric mind-twisting, numbing, subhuman issues one encounters in this unfortunate area of the law.

42

Insurance

Insurance factors have become increasingly important in the field of intellectual property litigation. Until a few years ago, little thought was given to the concept that insurance defense had anything to do with litigation between business competitors. Insurance was generally viewed as relating to negligence and property or personal injury. That, of course, is still the predominant area of insurance coverage and defense.

Today, however, the advertising injury provisions of a number of business policies have language that has opened the door to insurance coverage of, or at least a duty to defend, claims involving business torts or business-related causes of action. This has been particularly true of certain intellectual property causes of action.

The policy provisions that have opened the door often contain language that relates to such issues as unfair competition, false advertising, trade libel, and piracy. Sometimes the policies include trademark, copyright, false designation of origin, and trade secrets. Sometimes the policies specifically exclude such specific causes of action. It is not unusual for a policy to include unfair competition but exclude trademark. The irony of that kind of exclusion/inclusion provision is that in California, unfair competition has been held to be common-law trademark infringement, and statutory unfair competition has been held to be not covered by such policy language because there are no damages, only restitution (*Bank of the West v. Superior Court*, 2 Cal. 4th 1254, 10 Cal. Rptr. 2d 538 (1992)). Since restitution means the returning of something wrongfully taken, there is no insurance coverage and no duty to defend a wrongdoer's attempt to keep what he has no right to keep.

Following this reasoning, the only "unfair competition" that would appear to be covered is common-law trademark infringement. How does this square with the "no trademark coverage" language? There is no known answer to this question. It is merely posed to point out the kinds of esoteric considerations that are involved in trying to make legal and business judgments in this still somewhat murky area of the law.

In addition to the language found in the various policies, there are different interpretations placed on the duty to defend and the duty of coverage in different states. Thus, forum shopping is a fairly common practice for those seeking to obtain (or avoid) coverage and/or duty to defend.

It should be noted that the duty of coverage and the duty to defend are separate and distinct duties, although they are related. An insurance company may have a duty to defend, but not a duty of coverage. Under some types of policies, the duty to defend exists if the insurance company may have a duty of coverage (*CNA Casualty of California v. Seaboard Surety Co.*, 176 Cal. App. 3d 598, 222 Cal. Rptr. 276 (1986)).

When an insurance company denies that it owes a duty of coverage but it may be wrong, based either on the allegations of the complaint or what might later be alleged by amendment (based on the probable facts of the case), then it can still have a duty to defend. Some courts have even held that the inherent conflict of interest between the carrier (claiming no coverage) and the insured entitles the insured to its own lawyer, to be paid for by the insurance company (*San Diego Federal Credit Union v. Cumis Insurance Society, Inc.*, 162 Cal. App. 3d 358, 208 Cal. Rptr. 494 (1984)). This can be an enormous advantage to a small business that finds itself locked in litigation with a large, financially powerful competitor. More than one well-heeled plaintiff has been discomfited by discovering that its small adversary suddenly found a litigation treasure chest with which to defend itself. Sometimes this insurance treasure chest can also make the small party an effective counterclaimant as well.

Because of the enormous potential of insurance company defense funds to affect the outcome and even the existence of litigation, it is important that all affected and potentially affected parties consider the ramifications of insurance policy language. The affected parties include not only litigants and potential litigants but insurance companies as well. An unusual side effect of the development of this area of the law is that sometimes the insurance carriers become silent partners with their insureds in financing counterclaims in return for obtaining a share of the counterclaim as reimbursement for their attorney's fees.

From the carriers' perspective, their first consideration is whether they even want to sell policies that can pull them into litigation that can cost them millions in defense and possibly millions more in coverage. Unlike personal and property injury cases, where multimillion-dollar judgments are relatively rare, commercial litigation that involves gross sales often involves multimillion-dollar judgments. Because of the complexity of these cases, multimillion-dollar fees and costs are also not rare.

Many insurance companies sold such policies before the courts began holding that they created duties relating to intellectual property causes of action. There is also the question of whether the insurance companies felt these policies constituted a built-in immunity against coverage for willful torts, which would probably relate to false advertising, product disparagement, etc. They also may have felt that the vagueness of these provisions would shield them as well. It was probably suspicions of such motives that were behind the decision of the court in *CNA Casualty of California v. Seaboard Surety*, supra, wherein the California Court of Appeals held the insurance companies to a rather strict duty to defend.

Since that time a number of changes have been made in various policies, and there is really no such thing as standard intellectual property coverage language, although most such language is still found under advertising injury provisions. Also, the courts are more reluctant to hold that a duty exists (*Bank of the West*, supra). Nonetheless, such cases are still in existence, and as more becomes known about this area of the law, we can expect to see more such activity.

The two areas that seem to be hot spots for insurance activity are in the area of trademark law and patent infringement. The irony is that many policies expressly exclude both, and patent infringement often has been held not to arise out of advertising, even if it is piracy (*Bank of the West*, supra).

The reason patent infringement and trademark infringement give rise to coverage is because they are often associated with other causes of action that do trigger coverage. For example, an accused patent infringer may also be accused of false advertising for making claims about its alleged infringing product's being superior to the patent holder's product, by claiming that the patent holder is not the true inventor, or even of violating the antitrust laws by willfully infringing and engaging in other improper activities, such as false advertising, misappropriation of trade secrets, attempting to interfere with the patent holder's customers, and the like.

Such kinds of cases between competitors are not all that rare. Often such cases arise out of bad blood between competitors. Often they have had previous dealings with each other. One case that I tried involved a former exclusive distributor for a large company. The parties had a falling out when the distributor invented a product and tried to sell it. The company terminated the distributorship, infringed his patent, and then engaged in a series of acts that the jury and the court found to violate the antitrust laws and to be a tortious interference with a prospective business relationship. The result was a judgment of more than $20 million for the small company (*Automotive Products PLC v. Tilton Engineering, Inc.*, 33 USPQ 1065 (C. Dist. Cal. 1995)).

Ironically, the case was instituted by the large company, which sued to invalidate the patent and later added its own counterclaim of tortious interference. One can well imagine the duty to defend and coverage issues created by the various counterallegations.

From the insurance company's perspective, its concern is balancing the commercial value of providing a product (policy) that it can market as providing protection from intellectual property claims against the exposure and costs of defending such actions. What is somewhat puzzling is that most people who buy these policies don't usually even request these provisions. It's not uncommon for insureds to not even know they have such coverage, even after they have become involved in litigation. They don't discover the implications of their own policy language until after someone points it out to them. In other words, insurance companies often provide coverage that was never bargained for and yet that ends up costing them hundreds of thousands and sometimes millions of dollars in defense costs, even when it is ultimately decided that there is no duty of coverage.

Of course, an insurance company can always seek a declaratory judgment of no duty of coverage. If successful, it excuses the carrier of duty-to-defend costs. If unsuccessful, however, it means the carrier is on the hook for both defense costs and coverage. It has been my experience that most carriers don't seek a declaratory judgment, but rather pay the defense costs (sometimes on a reduced interim basis) and attempt to settle the issue later. By the same token, most claimants (or their lawyers) are willing to accept interim lower fees and defer the ultimate resolution of coverage and actual defense costs until later. These decisions are often driven by the facts in the underlying case. If the carrier feels the insured's liability is highly likely and the damages great, it may wish to push for a declaratory judgment action as soon as possible. Where liability is weak, the carriers are often ready to pay defense costs for a quick victory on the merits, if possible.

In terms of the initial strategic decisions, the carrier's first strategic decision should be not to sell a policy that subjects it to intellectual property duties of defense and coverage when the customer doesn't request them. It's amazing how many insurance agents don't even know such policy language is in their policies, much less what it means. From an insured's perspective, the first strategic decision should be to obtain the broadest possible coverage under the umbrella of "advertising injury." These policies are available, although more and more insurance companies are either omitting them or attempting to severely restrict their application. Before buying a business insurance policy, corporate counsel should always consult with an expert in this field. Failure to do so could result in the destruction of a company by legal costs alone.

The second strategic consideration from an insured's perspective is to check its policy immediately when and if it finds itself a defendant in any business litigation. Failure to tender the defense will result in waiver of all defense costs up until the time of tender. In addition, if the ultimate position of the defendant is jeopardized or compromised before tender, the insurance carrier may assert estoppel and refuse to be responsible for any defense costs or coverage. This, of course, is risky business for the carrier, which may be subject to allegations of bad faith, with the possibility of punitive damages, for jeopardizing its insured's position. This, incidentally, is one of the main reasons carriers will pay for a defense even when they have good reason to deny coverage. They can be held liable not only for attorney's fees and punitive damages but for derivative damages as well. If a company goes under because of defense costs that the carrier wrongfully refuses to pay, the carrier could be liable for the value of the entire business.

After the insured has reviewed its policy, if there is any possibility of coverage, the case should be tendered to the carrier. There is nothing to lose and a great deal to gain.

The possibility that a potential defendant may have such a policy is a strategic factor that also should be considered by a prospective plaintiff as well. In automobile accident and other personal injury and property injury cases, the plaintiff's lawyer's initial concern is whether there is a policy of insurance in effect that will make it possible to collect a judgment. If there is no such policy or if the limits are small, the case may not even be filed.

In business litigation, and particularly in intellectual property litigation, these concerns either may be nonexistent or may have just the opposite effect. (Of course, intellectual property plaintiffs like to collect judgments, and a defendant's policy may be an incentive to a plaintiff in some cases.) Often the intellectual property litigant is really interested only in an injunction. Also, since business competitors are the litigants, there is a good chance that a judgment may be collectible from the defendant. A plaintiff actually may desire to drive its opponent out of business and hopes the defendant isn't insured. In cases such as these, a plaintiff may very well wish to avoid triggering a potential defendant's policy. Triggering or not triggering one's opponent's policy often can depend simply on how a complaint is framed. A complaint for pure patent infringement usually will not trigger a policy (although some stouthearted souls still believe this is a possibility in some jurisdictions). A complaint for pure trademark or pure copyright infringement also may not trigger a policy (depending on the exclusionary language in the policy).

On the other hand, tying patent infringement or trademark infringement to another action may trigger at least a duty to defend. The worst scenario for a plaintiff is for a defendant's carrier to acknowledge its duty to defend and pay for a defendant's lawyer, but reserve its rights on coverage. This buys the defendant a defense but leaves collection of a judgment in limbo. Actually, the really worst-case scenario is when the defendant is able to use its insurance defense money to build a viable counterclaim against the plaintiff.

Of course, this insurance defense money issue cuts both ways. If the plaintiff has a policy that arguably applies to the defendant's counterclaim, the plaintiff may be able to tender its defense of its counterclaims to its carrier. Sometimes the carriers become silent partners in the counterclaims and agree to pay for them to get their fees back or as a backup to obtain coverage from the other side for their potential coverage to their insureds. We thus sometimes see the irony of two (or more) insurance companies stepping into the shoes of their respective insureds and doing battle with each other. One of the few certainties in life is that the salesmen who sold those policies never anticipated, in a million years, that this scenario would take place.

Accordingly, another strategic decision must be made by the defendant. It must ask itself if it wants to file a counterclaim that may trigger coverage for the original plaintiff.

To determine whether or not coverage or duty to defend may be triggered, one has to consider which types of action are most likely to bring about this result. Before *Bank of the West*, it was generally considered that "unfair competition" would be most likely to accomplish this result, at least in California, because the statute defines this so broadly that virtually any bad act in business qualifies. Since *Bank of the West*, however, this has become a weak reed because of the court's ruling that policies do not cover restitution. One cause of action that usually triggers coverage (and has replaced unfair competition as the tort of choice) is trade libel or product disparagement, since this is a damage claim arising directly from communication (and therefore qualifies as advertising injury). Accordingly, causes of action that can be linked into trade libel often can trigger coverage. In most states (e.g., California), the duty to defend part of the case becomes a duty to defend the entire case. In some other jurisdictions (e.g., New Jersey), some courts have apportioned attorney's fees between covered and noncovered actions.

A complaint for violation of the antitrust laws, tortious interference with a prospective business advantage, patent infringement, trade libel, or product disparagement, each being a separate count but each involving identical factual allegations, might very well trigger coverage. It would almost certainly trigger a duty to defend. Obviously, a plaintiff or counterclaimant could eliminate one or more of these causes of action (which may or may not be duplicative in their recovery—this is a very tricky area and must be navigated carefully) and thereby affect coverage and an opponent's ability to obtain a defense. Of course, this is not dispositive. The possibility of coverage, depending on the facts, may be enough for duty to defend (*Seaboard*, supra).

The bottom line is that a potential plaintiff and/or a potential counterclaimant should carefully analyze all the possible causes of action available to it, based on the complained-of conduct. Next, an evaluation should be made of the desirability of triggering coverage and/or duty to defend from your opponent's policy, if it has one. Finally, the various causes of action should be drawn to either trigger or not trigger a possible right under the insurance policy. There is some considerable guesswork involved, but those familiar with policy language should be able to cover the bases. Once the litigation is under way, the other side's policies can be obtained through discovery, and a party can decide if it wishes to modify its positions at that point.

Insurance has introduced a whole new set of parameters to be considered in business litigation and intellectual property litigation, in particular. Insurance has been a lifesaver for some small businesses that often didn't even know they had this kind of protection.

Today's corporate business and intellectual property lawyers need to be fully aware of all the ramifications of insurance in business litigation. This means they also must be fully aware of all the causes of action that are related to one another, particularly in the area of intellectual property litigation. Knowledge of these areas can be of great benefit to the client. Lack of such knowledge can be a disaster.

Bear in mind at all times that a duty to defend any portion of the case is a duty to defend the entire case. For example, I am presently involved in defending a case in Seattle. The client is a Massachusetts company that was sued for patent infringement in Seattle. There is no doubt in my mind that the plaintiff, a Fortune 500 company, believed that my client could not possibly defend that action. My client is not only based in

Massachusetts, but is a small business owned and operated by a husband and wife.

We tendered the case to the insurance carrier, which, predictably, rejected coverage as well as any duty to defend. We were able to persuade the insurance company that it did have a duty to defend based entirely upon allegations in a different cause of action, not the patent cause of action. The cause of action for which there was a duty to defend contained allegations of trade libel. As a result, and much to the consternation of the insurance carrier, the insurance carrier is now paying for and defending a relatively complicated patent infringement suit as well as the other causes of action. As a result of this insurance involvement, our client, much to the surprise and, I'm sure, considerable consternation of the plaintiff, has been able to launch a full-blown defense as to all of the causes of action asserted against it.

43

The Gag Factor:
Costs, Expenses, and Attorney's Fees

If you don't read any other portion of this book, you will still have spent the money but you will have saved yourself valuable time. The only chapter in this book that you really need to read is this one.

The constant complaint that I hear from corporations involved in intellectual property litigation is the costs! In my opinion, most of these complaints are justified (except, of course, as they apply to me).

Among the onerous duties and responsibilities that I have assumed over the years in order to pay my taxes is that of occasionally auditing costs, expenses, and attorney's fees on behalf of insurance companies. I also have the unfortunate experience of having to perform the same exercise in a case where attorney's fees were actually awarded against my client and I had to review the other firm's bills.[1] What I have discovered, which I am sure is no surprise to you if you have any experience at all in this type of litigation, is that the attorney's fees and costs are horrendous. It is not at all unusual for a patent case or an antitrust case to have attorney's fees alone in the multiple millions of dollars.

The obvious question is, "Is all this necessary?" The answer, in most cases, is no. Runaway costs and expenses can often be avoided if there is proper involvement from the outset by the party. Usually the party is

---

1. Fortunately, we settled that case and my client didn't have to actually pay anything—undoubtedly a tribute to my lawyering skills.

represented in these cases by in-house counsel. Sometimes they are represented by outside counsel, in the role usually fulfilled by in-house counsel, which is the role of corporate counsel, legal advisor, etc. Sometimes that role is actually provided by officers of the corporation who are not lawyers, but often have some substantial background or experience in litigation.

The problem is that most people who do not regularly deal in intellectual property litigation are, frankly, somewhat intimidated by it. In addition, there is often a great deal at stake in these cases, and the person responsible, at the corporate level, does not wish to rock the boat or be accused of hamstringing the efforts of the lawyers. All of these are legitimate concerns. That does not mean, however, there is any need for carte blanche.

In my opinion, the biggest source of abuse, when it comes to attorney's fees, is the so-called "team effort." What that usually entails is putting together a team of lawyers to deal with any particular case. As the case grows and expands, the size of the team often grows and expands. The team usually consists of a senior lawyer, who is probably the one with whom the case originated in the first instance, followed by medium-level partners, senior-level associates, and a number of junior-level associates. Often a number of associates are assigned to work on different portions of the brief, and this involves, quite obviously, large duplication of effort and often results in fees, for relatively straightforward motions, of tens of thousands of dollars. The better practice, in my opinion, is for the senior lawyer, who should be aware of all facets of the case, to write the summary judgment motion in the first instance. While that person's hourly rate may be higher, the efficiency in having the person most knowledgeable about the case write the summary judgment motion far more than offsets the advantage of having people with lower billing rates writing the motion in the first instance.

My practice is to dictate a draft of the motion, and when it comes to filling in citations of law, I will often simply state the word "citation." Thereafter, I will have an associate pull up the case law that supports the proposition of law I have stated. The reality is that there is no shortcut to preparing dispositive motions. The lawyer who is going to try the case needs to know all of the details of the case as it progresses. One of the worst scenarios I have seen is where a number of associates and lower-level partners prepare a case for trial and then hand it to the senior-level trial lawyer a few days before the trial. No matter how skilled he or she is, no lawyer can properly deal with these cases if that lawyer has not lived with the case from the inception.

Another source of fee escalation is when new lawyers are brought into the case and each one of those new lawyers has to wade through thousands of documents to come up to speed on the case, all at the client's expense.

My recommendation is that before employing a law firm to represent one, it is best to interview a number of firms and find out such things as how many jury trials they've actually had (it's amazing how many lawyers pass themselves off as trial lawyers in this area of the law and have never tried a jury trial). I would inquire about the firm's policy regarding staffing, etc. I would also ask the various firms to give me an estimate on what the litigation would cost. I am well aware of the fact that many things are outside of the control of the lawyer, and therefore a precise budget is impossible. This does not mean, however, that a reasonable estimate cannot be made. An experienced lawyer should be able to anticipate many of the factors involved and should be able to give a reasonable budget. This budget should include the overall costs, as well as monthly costs.

As far as expenses go, probably the biggest single expense is experts. Accordingly, I would apply the same philosophy to experts as I would to lawyers. That is, interview a number of them, find out their credentials and whether or not they actually have credentials that relate to the specific technology involved (it's amazing how many "experts" have no real expertise in the specific subject matter of the case). I would then get an estimate of the work that the lawyers expect the expert to do and a projection from the expert as to what she expects the fees to be.

Depending upon the circumstances of the case, it may be desirable to have the lawyer give an outside estimate of all costs and fees, and if the costs and fees run beyond that, then the lawyer simply has to eat those fees and costs.

Obviously, a lot of the factors above will have to be based upon the relationship between the party and the lawyer as well as a number of other intangibles, including the nature of the technology, etc. Nonetheless, the fundamental principle is that the client is paying the bills and should have an intelligent awareness of what is involved in the case as well as some estimate as to what it is going to cost.

44

The State of Our Judiciary

This is my chance to editorialize. The state of our judiciary is a disgrace; we have too few judges and too many cases. The main problem today is the overload placed on our courts by making them courts primarily of criminal jurisdiction. The most egregious of these crimes relate to drugs. What has happened is that our federal courts have basically become drug courts.

With regard to drug cases, there is really no reason they should be in federal court in the first place. There is absolutely no reason why state criminal justice systems can't deal with their own drug problems. The same applies to many of the diversity jurisdiction actions. There is no reason why those cases can't primarily be handled in the state where the cause of action arose.

A large share of the responsibility lies with U.S. attorneys who routinely file drug cases and other cases by the score, thus burdening an already bursting-at-the-seams judicial system. Congress seems to think that our federal judiciary should be a dumping ground for any number of causes of action. It seems that not a day goes by without Congress coming up with some new cause of action to be dumped in the federal courts, without any corresponding increase in the number of judges and staff sizes.

In addition, we have far too many politicians playing far too many games with judicial appointments. When Clinton was president, Orrin Hatch, the chairman of the Judiciary Committee, refused to even grant hearings on many of Clinton's appointments. Under the Bush Administration, we now have the Senate Democrats refusing to confirm a number of judicial appointments. In all fairness, the Republicans have been far more egregious in this matter than have the Democrats. The Republicans basically put a freeze on Clinton's nominations, particularly in Clinton's later years. The justices who have been rejected by the Democrats involve two high-profile appointments to the courts of appeals, both of which, arguably, involved ideological conservatives. In my opinion, the administration should concern itself primarily with appointing judges to the district court level, which is where the great need exists. For example, there are currently a vast number of vacancies existing in the Southern District of California. The Bush Administration has submitted a couple of nominations, but nowhere near enough.

With regard to the courts of appeals selections, every effort should be made, by any administration, to appoint people to those courts who carry no ideological baggage whatsoever.

The third problem is the salaries we pay judges. Those salaries are woefully inadequate, and as a result, it is difficult to attract good people to the federal judiciary. I believe that a number of federal judges exhibit a lackadaisical attitude toward their responsibilities because of the low pay. I know several of them who refuse to work on weekends, take off every federal holiday, and spend as much time as possible at federal judicial conferences, which, in my opinion, are a complete waste of time and the taxpayers' money. Many judges I know justify their conduct by the fact that they are paid so little.

The primary responsibility for this mess lies with the bar. We lawyers remain pitifully silent while our federal judiciary is in the process of self-destructing. Because my practice is exclusively limited to federal courts, I see this every day. Trying to get a case to trial and the constant delays, including sometimes more than a year for resolution of a summary judgment motion, is a source of never-ending frustration to the clients as well as those of us who practice in this arena. In the Federal Court for the Eastern District of Virginia, over the entranceway it states: "Justice Delayed is Justice Denied." That court breaks its neck to expedite these cases and finish them within six months. There is no reason why the other courts in this land, if properly staffed, can't do the same thing.

Finally, there should be the ability to remove federal judges for cause, not just impeachment. For example, Congress could establish guidelines and rules by which judges must abide. Any judge who delays more than six months in ruling on a motion for summary judgment should be subject to removal from the bench. Any judge who does not get a case to trial within a year and a half should be subject to removal. Any judge who does not rule on a simple motion (other than a dispositive motion, such as a summary judgment) within one month of the hearing should be subject to removal. That does not mean that these removals should be automatic, but the burden should be on the judge to establish good reason as to why these deadlines have not been met. As it stands right now, there is absolutely no leverage that anyone can bring to bear on these judges other than embarrassing them, as was done for some time by Senator Joseph Biden, who published a list of judges who inordinately delayed moving cases. His list was woefully inadequate, and the time limit given by him was far greater than should have been allowed. There should be a provision in the law to force judges to take action on cases and not delay them without excuse. Finally, federal judges should be instructed on the importance of being courteous to the lawyers who appear before them. Continued discourtesy by a federal judge should be grounds for some sanctions, if not removal from the bench.

In short, our federal judiciary is in need of wholesale revision, and this revision should start with Congress. The driving force behind bringing our federal judiciary into line with what it should be needs to come from the bar. As it stands right now, the bar remains basically silent on this issue. As a result, there is no pressure being brought on Congress or the judiciary to deal with the problems, which are not only not being resolved, but are, in fact, increasing at an alarming rate.

Please do your part in contacting your bar associations (including the American Bar Association) and contacting your senators and the White House to let them know that there is a crisis and that we, the members of the bar, intend to see it resolved.

45

Checklist of Causes of Action

Before filing a complaint or a counterclaim in these cases, you should think carefully of all the potential affirmative defenses and causes of action. A partial checklist follows.

- ☐ Patent Infringement
- ☐ State Unfair Competition
- ☐ Tortious Interference
- ☐ Federal False Advertising
- ☐ Trade Libel
- ☐ Defamation—false accusations
- ☐ Antitrust
- ☐ Copyright Infringement
- ☐ Trademark Infringement
- ☐ Trade Dress Infringement
- ☐ State and Federal False/Designation of Origin
- ☐ Patent Invalidity
- ☐ Trademark Invalidity

☐   Copyright Invalidity

☐   Laches

☐   Estoppel

46

The Final Chapter

Aha! I caught you! You have turned to the final chapter first, to see if it's worthwhile reading this book at all. You are probably the same person who turns to the last page of the murder mystery to see "whodunit" before you start reading the book. Of course, once you know, there is no sense reading the book, and this is why you never finished reading a mystery novel in your life. Maybe, by now, you should catch on.

In any event, I am not going to help you out. If you want to know what is in this book, you have to go back and labor through it the hard way, the way everyone else did.[1]

Now, for those of you who have actually suffered through this book, on behalf of myself, my mother, and intellectual property lawyers everywhere, I want to thank you for your kindness, your patience, your perseverance, your attitude, and your money.

I hope you have enjoyed reading this book. If you have and you let me know, I might even write another one on something that you can actually use. (This last sentence was part of the first book. Since no one told me they enjoyed reading it, I decided to write this sequel, which is of no use whatsoever.)

Bon voyage! Adieu! Adios! And may the wind be always at your back.

---

1. Come to think of it, everyone else didn't, but at least you could respect the effort that my staff put into this epic.

Table of Authorities

Federal Cases

State Cases

Docketed Cases

Federal Statutes

Appendix A

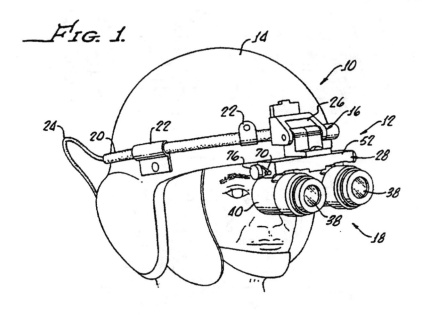

FIG. 1.

FIG. 2.

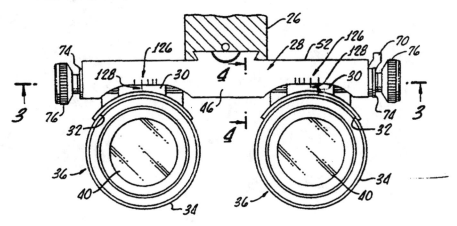

FIG. 3.

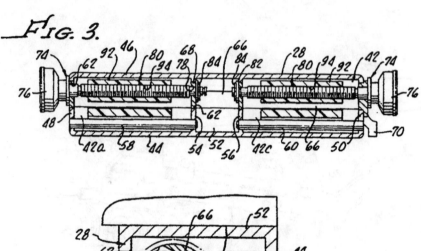

FIG. 4.

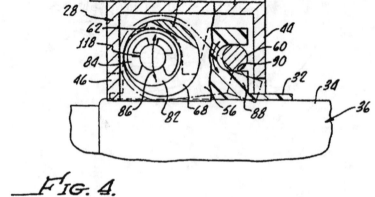

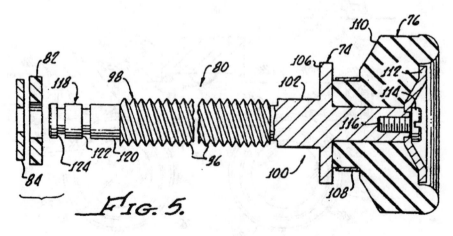

FIG. 5.

5,361,162

1

NIGHT VISION DEVICE

BACKGROUND OF THE INVENTION

1. Field of the Invention

The present invention relates to a vision device, particularly to a night vision device. More particularly, the present invention relates to a night vision device of the ANVIS (aviator's night vision imaging system) type, including a pair of monocular night vision scopes which are mounted and associated with one another in such a way as to provide the user of the device with binocular vision, thereby allowing the user to enjoy a night-time view with depth perception.

2. Description of Related Art

A conventional binocular ANVIS night vision device is depicted in U.S. Pat. No. 4,449,787, issued 22 May 1984, to James Burbo, et al, (the '787 patent) in which a pair of monocular night vision scopes are carried upon a mounting assembly. This mounting assembly provides for vertical adjustment of the monocular night vision scopes, as well as their adjustment for tilt, eye relief, and symmetrical interpupillary distance of the user.

A deficiency of the night vision device taught by Burbo in the '787 patent is that the user of the device must symmetrically adjust the monocular night vision scopes to provide a proper interpupillary distance so that the user enjoys binocular vision and depth perception. Unfortunately, the helmet or face plate which carries the night vision device may not naturally set on the user's head centered between the user's eyes. Such may be the case for a variety of reasons including individual variations in the helmets used, as well as non symmetries of the user's head conformation. In this case, the user of the night vision device will not be able to achieve a completely satisfactory adjustment of the monocular scopes to provide binocular vision and depth perception.

In addition, as the helmet or face plate settles during a period of wearing, shifts about slightly with the movements of the user, or with vibrations of the helicopter or other aircraft on which the user is riding, the user will be distracted as the quality of binocular vision and depth perception changes. This variation in view can be very distracting in the stressful environment in which such night vision devices are used. The human factors engineering of devices which are to be used in such high stress environments where the safety of flight operations can be affected not only by the utility of a device but also by how convenient and easy to use, or "user friendly", the device is, can easily be appreciated

Another ANVIS type of device which provides a night time view using both of the user's eyes and which provides for individual adjustment of interpupillary distance is seen in U.S. Pat. No. 4,463,252, issued 31 July 1984, to T. M. Brennan, et al, (the '252 patent). However, a night vision device according to the '252 patent includes only a single image intensifier assembly. The view provided to each of the user's eyes is a respective right or left half of the image provided by this singular image intensifier assembly. Consequently, the device according to the '252 patent cannot provide true binocular vision with depth perception.

Yet another conventional binocular night vision device is known as the ANVIS 6 in which a pair of night vision monoculars are suspended in front of the user's eyes by a frame which is rectangular in plan view. The frame is supported from a face plate or helmet which

2

the user wears in order to support the weight of the night vision device. The conventional ANVIS 6 includes an interpupillary distance adjustment mechanism with a pair of transversely aligned rotatable shafts, each drivingly coupled to the other at adjacent ends thereof, and each extending within the rectangular frame above one of the monocular scopes. Each shaft defines a respective thread portion of opposite hand, and the rectangular flame slidably carries a pair of depending monocular mounts each threadably engaging one of the threaded shafts. One of the threaded shafts includes an outwardly projecting knob rotation of which rotates both shafts and simultaneously moves the monocular mounts symmetrically together or apart to adjust interpupillary distance to the preferences of the user.

The conventional ANVIS 6 also includes a tilting mechanism which includes an elongate eccentric bushing device which is rotatable in the rectangular frame. This rotatable bushing carries the threaded shafts of the interpupillary adjustment mechanism, and moves these shafts in an arcuate path to tilt the monocular mounts relative to the rectangular frame about a slide and pivot shaft which is carried also by this frame.

With the interpupillary adjustment mechanism of the ANVIS 6, the user is also constrained to a symmetrical positioning of the night vision monocular. Also, each of the monocular mounts must be a separate piece, as are the two threaded shafts. This requirement for separate pieces increases the manufacturing costs of the ANVIS 6, while also increasing the logistics burden for repair and maintenance of the device.

SUMMARY OF THE INVENTION

In view of the above, a primary object of the present invention is to provide an ANVIS type of binocular night vision device with a pair of night vision monocular scopes and in which the night vision monoculars are individually adjustable for interpupillary distance relative to the user's head and eyes.

Another object of the present invention is to provide such a night vision device in which the interpupillary distance adjustment mechanism provides for non symmetrical placement of the night vision monocular relative to the user's head.

Still another object for the present invention is to provide a night vision device allowing independent interpupillary adjustment of the night vision monocular scopes relative to one another.

An additional object for this invention is to provide a binocular night vision device in which the interpupillary adjustment mechanism employs the same parts at both the left and right eyes of the user.

Yet another object for this invention is to provide a night vision device of the above-described character in which the interpupillary adjustment mechanism uses a pair of parts both made to a single part design at both the left and right sides of the mechanism, which single part by its design adapts the part for two different installations so that the tilting mechanism of an otherwise conventional ANVIS 6 night vision device is preserved with the use of the present invention, while at the same time allowing non symmetrical placement of the night vision monocular.

Another object is to provide apparatus supporting a monocular vision device relative to a user's head and eyes and which allows the vision device to be suspended in front of either of the user's eyes according to

5,361,162

3

preference and to be latterally adjustable for allignment with the preferred eye of the user.

Accordingly, the present invention provides a night vision device with a frame supported relative to a user's head and eyes, a pair of night vision monocular scopes depending from the frame in front of the user's eyes, and means for non symmetrical interpupillary adjustment of said monocular scopes relative said frame.

More particularly, the present invention provides an ANVIS 6 night vision device with an interpupillary adjustment mechanism allowing independent lateral positional adjustment of the night vision monocular scopes of the device relative to the user's head and eyes.

Still more particularly, the present invention provides an ANVIS 6 type of night vision device with the above described independent positional adjustment capability of the night vision monocular, which independent adjustment capability is achieved with use of the same adjustment parts at both the right and left sides of the device, thereby reducing the number of separate part designs required for the device.

Additional objects and advantages of the present invention will be apparent from a reading of the following description of a particularly preferred exemplary embodiment of the invention taken in conjunction with the following drawing Figures, in which:

BRIEF DESCRIPTION OF THE DRAWING

FIG. 1 is a fragmentary perspective view of a human wearing a helmet upon which is carried a night vision device;

FIG. 2 is a rear view of the night vision device seen in FIG. 1;

FIG. 3 is a partial cross sectional view taken along line 3—3 of FIG. 2;

FIG. 4 is an enlarged cross sectional view taken at line 4—4 of FIG. 3; and

FIG. 5 is an exploded and partially cross sectional view of components of the device seen in the other drawing Figures, and is presented at a considerably enlarged scale in order to better depict details of construction.

DESCRIPTION OF A PREFERRED
EMBODIMENTS

FIG. 1 shows a human 10 wearing a night vision system 12 which includes a helmet 14, a night vision device mount 16, and a night vision device 18. The night vision device mount 16 includes a halo-like structure 20 which is secured to the helmet 14 by plural spaces apart brackets 22. A power source (not shown) is connected with the mount 16 by a cable 24, and provides electrical power to operate the night vision device 18. Mount 16 also includes a centrally located bracket 26 which provides for vertical adjustment of the night vision device 18 relative to the helmet 14. Those ordinarily skilled in the pertinent arts will recognize that the helmet 14 is only one of several alternative support devices which the user 10 may employ to support the night vision device 18 in front of the user's eyes. For example, the user could just as well use a face plate or skull pad type of support device, both of which are well known in the pertinent arts, both of which are fully equivalent to the helmet 14 in respect to support of the night vision device 18. The night vision device 18 includes a frame 28 which secures to and depends from the central bracket 26. This frame 28 is of latterally elongate rectangular shape in plan view, and is also of

4

generally rectangular shape in both frontal and side elevation views. Depending from the frame 28 is a pair of spaced apart mounts 30 (best seen viewing FIG. 2), which at their lower extent define saddle-shaped receptacles 32 for receiving the cylindrical outer surface 34 of respective night vision monocular scopes 36. As FIGS. 1 and 2 in conjunction depict, the night vision monocular 36 at their forward ends each include an objective lens 38 by which low level light from a nighttime scene is received. At their aft ends, the night vision monocular scopes 36 each include a respective eyepiece 40 from which they provide to the user 10 an intensified image of the night-time scene.

In order to allow adjustment of the horizontal spacing between the monocular scopes 36 to match the interpupillary distance of the user 10, as well as allowing tilting of these scopes together in a vertical plane, the frame 28 defines a downwardly open recess 42, which is best seen viewing FIG. 3. This recess 42 is cooperatively defined by front, back, left, and right side walls, referenced with the numerals 44, 46, 48, and 50, respectively, which depend vertically from a top wall 52. A pair of centrally located and spaced apart interior partition walls 54, 56 divide the recess 42 into subparts which are referenced with the numerals 42a, 42b, and 42c.

Near the front of the frame 28, the partition walls 54, 56, in respective cooperation with the side walls 48, 50 carry a pair of slide and pivot shafts 58, 60, in the recess parts 42a, and 42c. In order to illustrate that each of the side walls 48, 50, and partition walls 54, 56, defines a respective one of four aligned bores (each referenced with the numeral 62), the side wall and partition wall at the left side of the frame 28 have been sectioned down to these bores as seen in FIG. 3.

Rotatably received in the bores 62 is an elongate eccentric bushing member 64. This bushing member 64 includes a thin elongate blade portion 66, and four eccentric bushing portions, each referenced with the numeral 68. The bushing portions 68 are received rotatably in the bores 62. To locate the bushing member 64 laterally in the frame 28, a pivot lever portion 70 of the bushing member 64 extends outwardly of the frame 28, and defines a shoulder 72 bearing externally on the side wall 50. A flange portion 74 of a right-side control knob assembly 76R captures the pivot lever 70 between the flange portion 74 and the wall 50. Similarly, at the left side of frame 28, a flange portion 74 of a respective left-side control knob assembly 76L bears against the left side wall 48. Consequently, the eccentric bushing member 64 cannot move out of the bores 62.

Rotatably received in respective left and right pairs of the bushing portions 68 of the bushing member 64 at aligned bores 78 thereof is a pair of essentially identical control shaft assemblies 80L and 80R. These control shaft assemblies respectively include the control knobs 76L and 76R. The aligned bores 78 are located eccentrically with respect to the bushing portions 68. In the recess portion 42b, each control shaft assembly 80 carries a washer member 82 which is secured axially on the control shaft by an E-type of retaining ring 84. In order to control friction levels in the mechanism, the washers 82 are preferably made of a polymer material with an inherently low coefficient of friction and good dry lubricity. Preferably, the washers 82 are fabricated of polytetrafluoroethylene, commonly known under the name, Teflon. Alternatively, a Nylon, Delrin, or other type of lubricous polymer material may be used in

5,361,162

5

making the washers 82. The washer members 82 bear on the respective bushing portion 68 of the bushing member 64 to prevent the control shaft assemblies 80 from moving outwardly of the bores 78.

Additionally, the washer members 82 are of sufficient diameter that they bear also on the respective partition walls 54, 56, to prevent the eccentric bushing member 64 from moving laterally in the frame 28. Consequently, lateral forces on the control shaft assemblies are transferred by the flanges 74 and washers 82 to the respective side and partition walls, and the eccentric bushing member 64 need not transfer these lateral forces through the thin elongate blade portion 66. However, it should easily be understood that the entire eccentric bushing member 64 is rotatable in the frame 28 in order to move the control shaft assemblies together through an arcuate path 86, which is best seen viewing FIG. 4. The thin elongate blade portion 66 of the eccentric bushing member 64 is easily able to sustain the torque required for this pivotal movement, and a pin portion (not shown) extends from the pivot lever 70 into an arcuate slot of the frame 28 to limit the extent of this pivotal movement to about eighty degrees of arc.

As is best understood by viewing FIGS. 3, 4, and 5 in conjunction, the night vision device 18 includes a pair of essentially identical mounts 30 which are slidably movable and are pivotal in the frame 28 on the slide and pivot shafts 58 and the control shaft assemblies 80. That is, each mount 30 includes a forward laterally elongate boss portion 88 which defines a laterally elongate and forwardly opening slot 90. The bosses 88 are slidably and pivotally received on the respective one of pins 58, 60 to allow substantially only sliding and pivoting motion relative to the frame 28. In other words, the fit of pins 58, 60, in the slots 90 is sufficiently close that side to side rocking of the mounts 30 does not occur.

Rearwardly of the boss 88, each mount includes a rear boss 92, which defines a laterally extending threaded bore 94 threadably receiving the control shaft assembly 80 at a thread defining portion 96 thereof. Because each of the control shaft assemblies 80 are substantially identical, the bores 94 are each provided with a tread of the same hand. Preferably, the hand of the thread portion 96 and of bore 94 is right-handed. Thus, it is easily understood that the mounts are movable laterally for interpupillary positional adjustment by rotation of the respective control knob 76. Additionally, the mounts 30 are pivotal together by pivoting of the lever portion 70.

Attention now to FIG. 5 in particular will show that each of the essentially identical control shaft assemblies 80 includes an elongate shaft portion 98 which defines the thread portion 96. The thread portion 96 of each of the control shaft assemblies 80 defines a multi-start thread of the same hand so that the mounts 30 on both the left and right side of the frame 28 are essentially the same. That is, these mounts are made to the same design and include bores 94 threaded with the same hand of multi-start thread to match the thread portions 96 of the control shaft assemblies 80. Adjacent to one end of the thread portion 96, the shaft portion 98 includes an integral collar 100 of enlarged diameter which defines both a bearing surface 102 which is rotatable in a respective one of the bores 78 of eccentric bushing member 64, and a shoulder 104 against which a washer member 106 is captured. The washer member 106 defines the flange portion 74 for the control knob assembly 80. The remaining parts of the control knob assembly 80 include a

6

spacer 108 which is interposed between the washer member 106 and a molded elastomer traction disk 110. This traction disk along with a retaining member 112 and the engagement of the traction disk with spacer 108 provides torque transfer from a user's fingers to the shaft portion 98. A screw 114 is threadably received into an axial bore 116 to capture the washer member 106, spacer 108, traction disk 110, and retention member 112, on the shaft portion 98. At its end opposite the control knob assembly 80, the control shaft portion 98 defines a reduced diameter stem portion 118. This stem portion 118 defines a bearing surface 120 which is rotatably received in a respective one of the bores 78 of the bushing member 64. Beyond the bearing surface 120, the stem portion 118 defines a pair of spaced apart grooves 122, 124, either one of which may receive the E-ring clip 84.

In order to compensate for the thickness of the lever portion 70 of the bushing member 64 at the right-hand side of the frame 28, the control shaft assembly 80 is installed with the E-ring clip 84 in the groove 124. On the other hand, on the left-hand side of the frame 28, an identical control shaft assembly 80 is installed with the E-ring clip 84 in the groove 122. Thus, the identical control shaft assembly by its configuration allows its installation in either one of two alternative configurations. Also, the control shaft assemblies 80 are identical on each side of the frame 28 so that the mounts 30 may also be the same. The result is a significant decrease in the manufacturing costs for the night vision device 18, as well as a reduction in the number of different parts required to be kept on hand for maintenance and service of the device.

In view of the above, it is easily understood that the interpupillary distance defined between the centers of the eyepieces 40 is adjustable by turning the control knobs 76. Additionally, this interpupillary distance need not be symmetrically arranged on either side of the center of the frame 28. That is, if the user 10 wishes, the interpupillary distance between the monocular scopes 36 may be asymmetrical relative to the frame 28 and the helmet or face plate which the user wears to support the night vision device. Thus, in those instances where the helmet or other support device does not repose in a position centered with respect to the user's eyes, the user nevertheless can achieve a satisfactory positioning of the monocular scopes 36, and resulting binocular vision. In order to assist the user in this respect, the frame 28 at its rear surface (best seen in FIG. 2) defines respective left-eye and right-eye indicia, indicated with the arrowed reference numeral 126, while the mounts 30 include an index mark 128. By use of these indicia and marks, the user 10 may adjust the interpupillary distance and non symmetrical disposition of the scopes 36 relative to the frame 28.

While the present invention has been depicted, described, and is defined by reference to a particularly preferred embodiment of the invention, such reference does not imply a limitation on the invention, and no such limitation is to be inferred. The invention is capable of considerable modification, alteration, and equivalents in form and function, as will occur to those ordinarily skilled in the pertinent arts. For example, because the invention as depicted and described is particularly adapted to provide the apparatus and structural advantages of the invention with an ANVIS 6 type of night vision device, a pair of the parts shown in FIG. 5 (i.e., the control shaft assemblies 80), along with one addi-

5,361,162

7

tional mount member 30 having a right-hand thread (one of the original mounts of an ANVIS 6 already being provided with a right-hand thread, while the other mount has a left-hand thread) could be employed as a retrofit kit for presently existing ANVIS 6 binocular night vision devices. Also, the invention may be used to support a viewing device for day or night viewing and of monocular type in front of a user's left or right eye according to preference. This leaves the user's other eye unobstructed for normal unaided sight, while the invention provides for very convenient lateral adjustment of the monocular viewing device for best alighnment with the user's preferred eye. That is, the invention may be used with only one of two possible monocular scopes mounted to the frame so that the other eye of the user is unobstructed, and the monocular scope is easily adjustable laterally relative to the user's preferred eye.

The depicted and described preferred embodiment of the invention is exemplary only, and is not exhaustive of the scope of the invention. Consequently, the invention is intended to be limited only by the spirit and scope of the appended claims, giving full cognizance to equivalents in all respects.

What is claimed is:

1. A viewing apparatus comprising:

a frame for being supported relative to a user's head and eyes;

said frame supporting a pair of night vision monocular scope mounts for lateral relative movement;

said pair of scope mounts carrying a respective left-eye and right-eye night vision monocular scope disposed in front of said user's eyes for cooperatively providing binocular vision, and defining therebetween an interpupillary distance;

said frame carrying means for laterally moving and positioning said monocular scope mounts relative to said frame to adjust said interpupillary distance, said moving and positioning means including a pair of respective laterally-extending threaded shaft members journaled by said frame and each threadably associated with a respective one of said pair of scope mounts to move the latter laterally of said frame in response to rotation of said shaft member, and said pair of shaft members being substantially identical with one another.

2. The invention of claim 1 wherein said pair of threaded shaft members each define a thread section of the same direction.

3. The invention of claim 1 wherein each of said pair of threaded shaft members includes an elongate stem portion journaled in said frame, said stem portion defining a circumferential groove, a washer member received on said stem portion adjacent a wall of said frame to bear thereagainst, and a clip member engaging said groove to trap said washer member between said clip member and said frame wall.

4. The invention of claim 3 wherein said washer member is of polymer material.

5. The invention of claim 4 wherein said polymer material is polytetrafluoroethylene.

6. The invention of claim 3 wherein said clip member is an E-ring type.

7. The invention of claim 3 wherein said stem portion defines a second groove like and spaced from said first-recited groove to define a pair of grooves.

8. The invention of claim 7 wherein one of said pair of shaft members is installed in said frame with said clip

8

member disposed in one of said pair of grooves, and the other of said pair of shaft members is installed with the clip member in the other of said pair of grooves.

9. The invention of claim 1 wherein said night vision device is an ANVIS 6 type.

10. The invention of claim 1 wherein said frame includes an interpupillary indicia disposed with respect to each of said pair of scope mounts, and each of said pair of scope mounts includes a respective index mark associated with said indicia.

11. A binocular night vision device comprising a frame supported relative to a user's head and eyes, a pair of night vision monocular scopes depending from said frame in front of the user's eyes, and means for non symmetrical interpupillary distance adjustment of said pair of monocular scopes relative to said frame.

12. The invention of claim 11 further including a pair of substantially identical laterally extending interpupillary distance control shafts journaled in said frame and threadably associating with a respective one of said monocular scopes.

13. The invention of claim 12 wherein each of said control shafts includes an elongate thread portion, a control knob assembly at one end of said thread portion, and an elongate stem portion at an opposite end of said thread portion, said elongate stem portion defining a pair of spaced apart grooves.

14. The invention of claim 13 wherein each of said pair of control shafts carries an washer member bearing axially against said frame, and a retaining clip member received in one of said pair of grooves.

15. The invention of claim 14 wherein said washer member is make of a polymer material.

16. The invention of claim 15 wherein said washer is made of polytetrafluoroethylene.

17. The invention of claim 14 wherein one of said pair of control shafts carries said clip member in one of said pair of grooves, while the other of said pair of control shafts carries said clip member in the other of said pair of grooves.

18. An ANVIS 6 type binocular night vision device with a pair of monocular night vision scopes cooperatively defining an interpupillary distance, and an interpupillary distance adjustment mechanism allowing independent lateral positional adjustment of the night vision monocular scopes of the device relative to a user's head and eyes.

19. The ANVIS 6 night vision device of claim 18 wherein said independent interpupillary distance adjustment capability is achieved with use of the identical adjustment parts at both the right and left sides of the device, thereby reducing the number of separate part designs required for the device.

20. A retrofit kit for an ANVIS 6 type of binocular night vision device including a frame supporting a pair of monocular night vision scope mounts, and a monocular night vision scope disposed on each of said mounts to cooperatively provide binocular vision with depth perception, said retrofit kit providing for independent positioning of said scopes relative said frame to cooperatively define an interpupillary distance between eyepieces of said scopes, which interpupillary distance may be asymmetrically disposed relative said frame, said retrofit kit comprising:

a pair of substantially identical interpupillary distance control shaft assemblies each adapted to be journaled by said frame and to threadably associate with a respective one of said scope mounts, each

5,361,162

9

control shaft having a thread portion of the same direction, and

a replacement scope mount adapted to replace one of said pair of scope mounts of said ANVIS 6 night vision device, said replacement scope mount having a threaded bore of the same direction and threadably engageable with one of said pair of control shaft assemblies.

21. A viewing apparatus comprising:

a frame for being supported relative to a user's head and eyes;

said frame supporting a monocular viewing device for being disposed in front of a selected one of said user's eyes, said frame further carrying means for laterally moving and positioning said viewing device to align the latter with said selected eye of the user, said moving and positioning means including a respective mount slidably carried on said frame for supporting said viewing device and a laterally-extending threaded shaft journaled by said frame, threadably engaging said mount to move the mount laterally in response to rotation of said threaded shaft and traversing only said selected eye of said user; whereby lateral movement of said viewing device to align with said selected user eye is independent of lateral movement of another such viewing device mount which may be carried by

10

said frame forwardly of the other of said user's eyes.

22. The invention of claim 21 wherein said frame carries a pair of said mounts each for being disposed forwardly of a respective eye of said user, and a pair of independent threaded shafts each journaled by said frame and threadably engaging a respective one of said pair of mounts.

23. The invention of claim 22 wherein said pair of threaded shafts are substantially identical with one another.

24. The invention of claim 22 wherein said pair of mounts are substantially identical with one another.

25. The invention of claim 22 wherein each of said pair of threaded shaft members includes an elongate stem portion journaled in said frame, said stem portion defining a circumferential groove, a washer member received on said stem portion adjacent a wall of said frame to bear thereagainst, and a clip member engaging said groove to trap said washer member between said clip member and said frame wall.

26. The invention of claim 25 wherein said stem portion defines a second groove like and spaced from said first-recited groove to define a pair of grooves.

27. The invention of claim 26 wherein one of said pair of shaft members is installed in said frame with said clip member disposed in one of said pair of grooves, and the other of said pair of shaft members is installed with the clip member in the other of said pair of grooves.

* * * * *

About the Author

Edward F. O'Connor is a patent attorney who specializes in intellectual property litigation. He is chairman of the Intellectual Property Department of Stradling Yocca Carlson & Rauth in Newport Beach, California. He received his Bachelor of Science degree in physics from the University of Michigan and his law degree from Indiana University, Bloomington.

Mr. O'Connor has tried numerous jury and nonjury intellectual property cases throughout the United States, as well as handling numerous appeals before the CAFC. He is a past chairman of the Intellectual Property Committee of the Tort and Insurance Practice Section of the ABA.

Index

A

abandonment 26
  and inequitable conduct 109
  unintentional 109
accounting records 41
advertising 40–42
anticipation 43–45, 87–90, 101, 135
  and doctrine of equivalents 88
  case findings 90
  defined 44
  test for 88
antitrust law 3–5
  and judicial safeguards 53
  and market analysis 5
  and market power 7
  and patent fraud 14
  and patents 19
Areeda, Phillip 8
attorney-client privilege 35–38, 61
  and written opinions 36
  correspondence 37
  patent litigators 37
  validity and infringement opinions 37
  waiver of 37

B

Berne Convention 174
Bork, Robert 5

C

Chicago School 5, 7
claim interpretation 45–47, 75–76, 85
  defining terms 76–77
claims
  analysis 63
  classes of 65
complaint allegations
  publication of 15

confidentiality 58
continuation application 115
  and submarine patents 116
continuation process 115–17, 119, 120
continuation-in-part application 115–17
contributory infringement 66–67
copyright
  concept of 169
  date of creation 173
  date of publication 173
  enforcement of 170
  fair use doctrine 178
  reasonable royalty 171
  registration of 11, 176, 179
  renewal provision 174
  software 11, 180–82
  treatment of restored 175
  works made for hire 179
copyright infringement 14, 15, 16
  copyright invalidity 183
  establishment of 177
  presumption of validity 184
copyright law 167–68, 187
  Sonny Bono amendment 187
copyright misuse 13
Copyright Office of the Library of Congress
  11, 13
copyright protection 169
  and piracy 170
  and the Internet 170
  Berne Convention 174
  cartoon characters 170
  length of time 172
  loss of 179
  music 177
  personal identities of celebrities 170
  work made for hire 173
copyright tying 10–12
  and market power 10
  and software 11
Court of Appeals for the Federal Circuit 10,
  44, 46, 54, 69, 72, 81, 105, 119